With God's Blessing and
a Green Beret

Grounds

HAZELDEAN
BATH Rd
STURMINSTER NEWTON
DORSET
DT10 1DS
Tel (0258) 472 224

With God's Blessing and a Green Beret

A Pilgrimage

by The Reverend Canon John Wallis, D.S.C., M.A.,
Canon Emeritus of Salisbury

Firebird Books

First published in the UK in 1994
by Firebird Books P.O. Box 327,
Poole, Dorset BH15 2RG

Copyright © 1994 Ruth Wallis

All rights reserved. No part of this
book may be reproduced or
transmitted in any form or by
any means, electronic or
mechanical, including photo-
copying, recording or any infor-
mation storage and retrieval sys-
tem, without prior permission in
writing from the copyright holder
and publisher.

ISBN 1 85314 200 X

Typeset, designed and produced
by Crispin Goodall Design Ltd,
463 Ashley Road, Parkstone,
Poole, Dorset BH14 0AX

Printed and bound in
Great Britain by Short Run Press
of Exeter

Foreword

The name John Wallis will strike a chord with those who remember him as Rector of Wareham in Dorset, but there are many hundreds of sailors who served in destroyers in the British Pacific Fleet who will have known him only as "Padre" or "The Bish". All his shipmates cannot fail to have happy memories of the tall black-bearded padre who was always ready to enter into the spirit of any off-duty fun and yet commanded respect when conducting a Church Service or attending to the welfare of the men he served with.

His Distinguished Service Cross, won while serving with the Royal Marines in Salerno, was well deserved: there can't be many padres with this award.

If an autobiography is a reflection of one's personality, you will enjoy getting to know John Wallis, with his lively sense of humour and deep devotion to duty.

Bill Johnson DSC

Contents

CHAPTER ONE

The Journey Begins

In a collection of reminiscences such as this, I suppose it is usual to begin with one's earliest memories. I believe my earliest memory takes me back to the time before I was born. As a youngster I had the most appalling nightmares: I knew that I had to do the impossible, a colossal, impossible task, as if I had to get over or through an unscaleable or impenetrable wall with water threatening all the time and there was no way of avoiding the task. I would wake up so terrified that I wanted to be sick. It was a ghastly experience.

I gradually left it behind me but it was some forty years before I understood what it was all about. Sitting next to the professor of psychology at dinner one evening at the college of Durham University where I was chaplain, the subject of dreams and nightmares came up for discussion and I mentioned this nightmare that used to plague me. The professor immediately said, "That was pre-natal, it goes back to your birth, the struggle to get out of your mother's womb". I managed this in 1912.

We lived in a small semi-detached house in Southampton, quite near to the Common. My father was a clerk in the Union Castle Steamship's Company offices in Canute Road, the youngest of a family of thirteen; my mother was one of a family of five. I had a sister two years older than I. I must have been three or four years old when I was taken to the railway station in my pushchair to see my father back to France. Just before he got into the train he gave me a French coin and kissed me good-bye. For some time afterwards each time I looked at or fingered this coin I wanted to cry; it was a pathetic reminder of his leaving us. A few years later when I returned from school one afternoon I remember the joy of my father's final homecoming.

Those 1914-18 war years brought many trials and tribulations to families and especially to mothers whose husbands were overseas. My sister and I went down with flu in the epidemic of 1918. My mother, feeling shaky herself, had to struggle up and down stairs. I recall her sobbing to herself on the stairs one morning. She had cut a boiled egg in half for our breakfast as she had often had to because food was in short supply. Unfortunately she had tripped and the contents of the tray had slid down the stairs.

It was in my first year at school, late in 1917 or more likely in 1918, at the time of the Bolshevik revolution, that we were asked to take to school for the poor Russian peasants any comforts we could spare. I remember wrapping a tin of cocoa in a navy blue woollen scarf as my contribution.

From time to time when the wind was in the right direction, we would hear the pounding of the guns across the Channel; at times during the battle of the Somme it seemed to be incessant. I remember feeling apprehensive one night on seeing a German zeppelin caught in our searchlights over the town. The bottom of our garden adjoined the grounds of a large mansion which housed German officer prisoners-of-war. Night after night I lay in my bed listening to the sentry taking a turn up and down, and sometimes hearing, "Halt, who goes there?"

One incident may be worth recording here in view of the eventual direction of my life. One Sunday morning my father, either home on leave from France, or just demobilized, was taking me for a walk: I couldn't have been more than five or six years old. I suppose my father had been to pay his respects at one of the family graves because my memory is of walking along beside the cemetery wall and asking him if the Germans had the same God as we had. It was something I couldn't understand.

Other wartime memories: an aeroplane, one of ours, hanging in an oak tree on Southampton Common; the marching of soldiers from the huge tented camp on the Common to the docks for embarkation to France, and then, at last, the Victory Parade of British, Australian, American and all nationalities, marching through the town's main street. A gigantic bonfire had been built on the Common for the evening's festivities but, unfortunately, some revellers had set it alight the night before.

When the occupants of the camp had eventually disappeared, the citizens were once more given their rights and we took the first opportunity of wandering around territory which, until then, had been forbidden to us. In 1946 when I was demobbed after the 1939-45 War, I had to go the NAAFI in the camp on the Common to collect my ration of cigarettes and tobacco. I was reminded of the 1914-18 War camp although Nissen huts had largely taken over from bell tents.

My grandfather was what used to be called a Jobbing Master, corresponding to a modern taxi hire firm. He had stabling in the town with a number of horses and all sorts of vehicles: brougham, landau, brake, pony trap. He had a flourishing business until the motor car took over and I can remember the sad day in 1926 when the business was sold up for next to nothing. He had been advised years before to get into motor cars but he was too conservative or pigheaded and reckoned the horse would never be replaced.

I used to enjoy those stables and the horses and sitting with the coachmen in the tack room, savouring the smell of leather harness which was, at times, outdone by the pungent but equally acceptable smell of the men's shag tobacco. I think it showed a reasonable liberalism on the part of my elders and betters to allow me at an early age to spend so much time with these chaps, although one day the elders were a bit cross because I had been ducked in the large horse trough which stood in the yard always full to the brim. I suppose I'd been cheeky. I picked up a bit of the language and I well remember trying it on my father one evening in the garden. He nearly exploded when I said, "Those are bloody good tomatoes!" "What did you say?" "I said those are jolly good tomatoes." "Oh," he said, and gave me a strange side-long look.

Some of the most vivid and happy memories are of the time I spent as a choirboy at our parish church. I can still remember the names of most of the boys who were choristers with me in 1922. By the grace of God, and perhaps it was my mother's influence, too, I seemed to take to religion and to the life of the church from an early age. I recall with what eagerness I waited to be collected to make my first attendance at Sunday school at the age of five. The

11

Christian faith grew on me and has remained the most important element in my life.

I think the cumulative effect of my years as a chorister was considerable: singing the psalms week after week, year after year; listening to the Prayer Book collects and to the reading of scripture. To many the repetition of so much of the Prayer Book liturgy may seem nothing but empty words, but after many years something of the meaning and the truth of those words takes root in us and becomes an important part of our life: the Word is once again made flesh.

At school I was academically mediocre: I failed the eleven plus exam but I was not a complete clot. Fortunately, my father sent me to a very good secondary school where I didn't shine at anything but received a useful education. I was a late starter. I left school in 1929 at the age of seventeen. One night at the youth club, the vicar of the parish made what was to me the extraordinary suggestion that I might consider becoming a parson. I was quite amused and told him I was more likely to become a purser because I had always hankered after the sea. The chance to get in touch with ships came unexpectedly in the summer of 1929 after I had taken the School Certificate with a few credits and a distinction in English. I managed to land a job in the catering department of the offices of the Cunard Steamship Company on the princely wage of ten shillings per week.

There was a staff of eight of us in the office and more in the docks. We were responsible for storing the liners with food and drink and, when there was a quick turnaround of the *Aquitania* or *Mauretania*, we could be at it till late at night, 'phoning and ordering, and preparing custom papers for the wines and spirits. The amounts of fruit and vegetables, meat, fish and poultry, etc, were astronomical. Some of it was obtained locally but a good deal came by rail from London. There were Hundreds of bottles of wines and spirits, beer and lager, thousands of packets of cigarettes and cigars and tobacco.

The company had its own bonded warehouse in the docks where it brewed its Bass, Worthington and lemonade. One of my colleagues in the office made out the warrants for all the wines that had to be shipped and one of my jobs was to get these warrants through Customs and then take them to the ship. This could sometimes be a rush job, especially if the barkeeper had rung up at short notice to say he wanted a few dozen more bottles of champagne or claret or what-have-you. I enjoyed this part of the job: it got me out and about which was far more to my liking than sitting on a stool in the office, adding up columns of figures, or checking barkeepers' accounts. For one thing I met all sorts of fellows in the Custom House.

One day, however, I was thoroughly ashamed of myself. I pulled out of my pocket a lighter to light my cigarette and the Customs clerk said what a nice lighter it was. I said he could have it for half-a-dollar, i.e. 2s 6d, and we did a deal. I had recently celebrated my 21st birthday and had been given three cigarette lighters. As I turned to the fellow standing next to me at the counter, I was shattered to find it was the man who had given me one of the lighters.

At the beginning of my career I frequently lost my way on the liners, looking for the Barkeeper's or the Chief Steward's office; it was like a rabbit warren two or three decks down but it was worth it because I was always offered a drink and I came to appreciate lager off the ice. I also enjoyed lunching on board but to begin with the size of the menu frightened me. I wish I had kept some of those menus from the early thirties. I doubt it any modern hotel could produce anything approaching such a selection. On a number of occasions I was fortunate to see some of the famous figures and film stars on their way to New York. I was vastly impressed by the height of Carnera, the boxer. Another enjoyable part of my duties was visiting the bottling store at East Warehouse in the docks; a bottle of Bass or Worthington was always on offer.

I found my work most congenial but the sporting activities offered by the firm really made life in those days before the war times to be remembered. I played in the second eleven at cricket which meant happy Saturday afternoons of village cricket in the New Forest, followed by the odd pint or two. Then in winter I played in the second eleven at soccer on a ground now part of Southampton Airport. After a shower and a good tea in what had been a 1914-18 War aeroplane hangar, we would spend some time playing brag or solo. On Friday night at the Victoria Rooms – the billiard

13

saloon of the town – a table was at our disposal. My youth was by no means misspent.

Although those were happy days for me, they weren't for many people. The crash on Wall Street was quickly followed by the slump in 1930. I can remember stevedores, stewards and dock labourers in their hundreds crowding round the dock gates hoping against hope that a job might turn up; it really was a sad sight. With the crash of the Royal Mail Lines everyone in shipping became apprehensive and reductions in salary had to be accepted by many. I felt safe on my ten shillings a week; in fact, after a year, I was given a rise to fifteen shillings a week.

CHAPTER TWO

Changing Direction

You will have formed the opinion that I was quite settled in the Cunard Line; I was and even found it a satisfying job but all the time I had a strange, uncomfortable feeling that it wasn't what I should be doing. I vaguely considered journalism and tried my hand at writing and even went to evening classes on the history of literature. I linked up with the Oxford Group and went to one of their house parties at Oxford in 1931. A question that was to worry me was: what is life for? What is the purpose of life? This may have been behind the feeling of disquiet that I was not doing what I was supposed to be doing.

Gradually things began to fall into place. After a small operation for the removal of tonsils and adenoids, I caught a chill which led to a bout of jaundice. I lost a lot of weight and was confined to bed for some weeks. When I managed to get out and about again, it was spring and nature was showing signs of life. This, combined with my recovery, brought to me an overwhelming sense of gratitude which spilled over into my religion. I felt so very grateful to God for giving me life and health and strength and happiness. In addition, it was in Lent that year that the sufferings and death of Jesus of Nazareth became for me very real indeed, so real that I felt myself personally involved and under an obligation to try to make it as true and real to others. There was no question of my making any decision, it was out of a profound sense of gratitude that I knew I had to spend the rest of my life trying to help others to accept the love and goodness of God, expressed for me as for many hundreds of people in the words of the hymn:

> "Were the whole realm of nature mine
> It were an offering far too small,
> Love so amazing, so divine,
> Demands my life, my soul, my all."

I suppose this conviction or call or religious experience had been creeping up on me for some time but it eventually came to me with tremendous force, not at a service in church but one evening when I was out with a typist from the Cunard Company's typist pool. When I arrived home, I was somewhat excited and I told my parents that I had to become a priest. I'm pretty sure my father thought I was a bit tight and all he said was, "You get on to bed and we'll talk about that tomorrow."

I was so full of this new-found experience that the next day at the office I couldn't keep quiet about it and was called a bloody fool and told that I obviously had religious mania. I rather enjoyed myself telling them that they knew quite well that I was as sane as they were. From then on my life became more straightforward as if I were living in a different direction.

My first move was to get in touch with the vicar of the parish, with whom I was not on the best of terms at that time. He foxed me by asking, "What about your spiritual life?" I was so ignorant on matters of the soul that I really hadn't a clue as to whether I had a spiritual life. I used to go to church and say my prayers and I wondered if that's what he was talking about.

I think my religion owed a great deal to Geoffrey Studdert Kennedy, the popular Army chaplain of the 1914-18 War, Woodbine Willie. I got a lot from reading his books, especially the collection of his verse, 'The Unutterable Beauty'. I read and re-read these poems and snippets of verse so that after a year or two I had most of them by heart. They have come in very handy down the years as quotations in sermons and talks and his cockney dialect verse has always gone down well in military circles. He had the ability to make Christian truth come alive. Another source of inspiration was the annual camp run by the Winchester Diocesan Youth Movement in the '30s when about a hundred teachers, nurses, etc. from Bournemouth and Southampton parishes spent a couple of weeks under canvas in Purbeck and then in North Wales until the War ended it all in 1939.

My parish priest gave me a decent write-up and put me in touch with the Bishop of Winchester, Cyril Garbett, who

16

thought I might do, but that I would have to matriculate before getting any further. I was wisely advised to take a Wolsey Hall Correspondence Course but having only the evenings and weekends to deal with this, it took me well over a year before I felt able to sit London Matric. This was probably the hardest grind of my career but the sheer discipline of coming home from a day's work and then getting down to an hour or so's study and having to forego outings with the lads stood me in good stead for the remainder of my student life. I managed the five subjects fairly comfortably.

After almost five years in the Cunard line, I put in one term at Southampton University College trying to get hold of some Latin and Greek and a touch of philosophy. I was once more enjoying life with freedom from books and spent many hours swimming and diving in the public baths at Southampton.

It must have been the result of too much diving that I developed ear-trouble and had to see the Ear, Nose and Throat consultant at the Royal South Hants Hospital, who promptly made me an in-patient and, after a couple of days, on a Sunday morning, I was whisked into the theatre for a mastoid operation. My most vivid memory of this episode was that as I lay on the operating table awaiting unconsciousness, I heard the Civic Centre clock chiming, 'O God our help in ages past', which it did every day at 12 noon. Isaac Watts, the writer of this popular hymn, had been a resident in Southampton.

In September that year, 1934, I entered St Boniface College at Warminster in Wiltshire to read for a Durham Licentiate of Theology (L.Th). I managed theology, Parts one and two, without much trouble but I had spent far too much time producing a play in the local theatre, which the college did each year, that I had to put in a further term to take my classics papers.

During the long vacation some theological students used to go on a mission to the Kent hopfields. It was called a mission but if the object was to take the Christian faith to the East Enders, I never felt I gave any of them much to write home about but it certainly broadened my already fairly wide experience of human nature – and my vocabulary! I

17

well remember on my return to College the following term reporting to the staff and students a few incidents and repeating verbatim the lurid language of the three bin-men who slept beneath us in the oast house where we had our quarters. The Principal was not amused.

I then went on as a L.Th. to Durham University to com-

plete my BA Degree, which required one further year only, although it called for assiduous study.

My first visit to Durham Cathedral was something I shall never forget: the sheer strength of the Norman architecture, especially the pillars in the nave. The great hall of Durham Castle, the dining hall of University College was shared by Hatfield College where I was in residence.

John as a young curate, Holy Trinity Trowbridge, 1939

The summer of 1938 was a worrying time; should I ever be ordained or would I be conscripted into HM Forces? I well remember in the long vacation taking my mind off the subject by spending an afternoon at the Flicks and going home on the 'bus and seeing the headline on the newspaper of the man in front of me, 'Peace in our Time'. The relief was tremendous. Recently, when I kept the fiftieth anniversary of my ordination to the priesthood, a contemporary rang to offer his congratulations and asked me if I remembered how worried we all were in that summer term of 1938, wondering if we would be ordained.

I was happy to confine my sporting activities to rowing and after drinking tea off the mantelpiece for some weeks I managed to cope with fixed seats which I was told was the only way to learn the art. The steam rising from bodies after a brisk row on a cold winter's morning on the River Wear

18

is a vivid memory, but the most wonderful memory is of finishing my exams with a three hour Modern History paper at 5pm and rushing to the station to catch the train to Edinburgh to row in the Torpids. Our coach had waited to make sure I caught the train and he insisted on my having two dinners of roast beef.

At the beginning of 1939 I was looking for a parish that wanted a curate and found one at Holy Trinity, Trowbridge, in Wiltshire and was made deacon by the Bishop of Salisbury on 3rd March, 1939. I spent two and a half happy years there. I became padre of the local branch of Toc H; we had a flourishing youth club; I coached the Bradford-on-Avon Fitzmaurice Grammar School Four on the river; fished now and then; and the countryside was ideal for walks along the Kennet and Avon Canal to Bradford-on-Avon, to Limpley Stoke, and to Bath. Many of my memories of those days were centred on the girl that I was to marry seven years later.

CHAPTER THREE

Service with
The Royal Marines

In May 1940 in preparation for my ordination to the Priest-hood, I had spent a few days in retreat at Glastonbury. On returning to the parish of Holy Trinity, Trowbridge, the first person I happened to meet was the Roman Catholic priest who was amazed to learn that I knew nothing of the failure of the Maginot Line and the German advance into Belgium and Holland. I had neither seen a newspaper nor heard the radio for some days.

Dunkirk and the following months were exciting. There was a barracks in our parish which until that time had housed a handful of officers, ten horses and less than one hundred men. Most weeks they filled half the Church at the Sunday morning parade service. Very soon the barracks was bursting at the seams with survivors from Dunkirk and tents were put up on every available inch of ground around the barracks. That summer we lived in daily expectation of inva-sion and we were thrilled at the battles going on over our heads.

In 1941 I began to get a bit restless and to feel that I ought to be serving in some way, other than, and more useful than that of a curate in Wiltshire. I asked the Bishop of Salisbury if I might join the Royal Navy but he said the parishes as well as the Services needed young men. After some months I went to see his assistant, the Bishop of Sherborne who was a little more sympathetic and who was a friend of The Venerable Thomas Crick, Chaplain of the Fleet at that time.

As a result I was summoned to the Admiralty for an inter-view and a medical. This was followed by an appointment to HMS *Drake* at Plymouth on 11th June 1941. I was fortu-nate in missing the really heavy raids on Plymouth although on most nights the sirens took us all to our shelters. It was a useful few weeks getting the atmosphere and the taste of the Navy and picking up the main features of the job of a

Naval Chaplain; daily prayers, usually on the parade ground, a daily visit to the sick bay and to the cells, Sunday morning worship in the base Church, and visiting ships in the dockyard. I exhibited my immaturity in HMS Kent by tripping and falling headlong over a lead.

There were a number of Cruisers in Devonport for repairs or a refit at that time and I thought I might have been fortunate enough to be appointed to one. Instead I was sent to join the Royal Marines in South Wales, to a hutted camp just vacated by a Belgian battalion at Penally near Tenby in Pembrokeshire. Space appeared to be a bit short but the Adjutant managed to find enough room for me to put up my camp bed and my canvas wash basin in what I think was intended for a cycle shed. I was thankful that I had my sleeping bag and camping equipment with me. During this short stay at Penally I was told I was entitled to claim hard-lying money. I mention this because it came as such a surprise; I wonder why the cold and wet and the mud of the winter of 1941-42 on Woodbury Common, didn't yield the same benefit? Not that we ever gave it a thought in those days.

John's identity Certificate as chaplain R.N.V.R

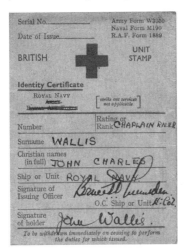

My stay at Penally was very short indeed, so short that I wondered if someone had made a mistake in my appointment. After a few days I received a posting to serve as Chaplain to 7th Battalion Royal Marines on Woodbury Common, Devonshire but as there was no accommodation yet at this camp which became known as Dalditch, I was to be attached to Lympstone, which then consisted of a number of wooden hutments which may well have been hang-overs from the 1914-18 War. It was the H.Q. of 103rd brigade. Being somewhat new to service rules and regulations and discipline and as my journey by rail from South Wales to South Devon could conveniently pass through Trowbridge, I decid-

21

ed I would break my journey and see something of my friends and parishioners and spent a night in my former digs. The following day I found my way down to Exeter and out to the Camp on Woodbury Common, arriving in the early evening. The C.O. greeted me warmly. "We thought you were coming yesterday" he said, "come and have a glass of beer".

After a short spell at Brigade H.Q. at Lympstone a bell tent was provided for me under some fir trees near the entrance by the 8th Batt. lines on Woodbury Common. Some of the officers lived out in East Budleigh or Exmouth and some of us in bell tents well into the late autumn. It was pleasant enough, especially the scent of the fir trees, but our clothing in trunks and suitcases tended to get damp and our uniforms creased. Fortunately the incipient officers' mess at least had a concrete floor to it but only canvas walls and roofing. At times it was rather chilly in the evenings. After some months Nissen huts were built and roads were laid down but the mud of that 1941 autumn and early winter was to be seen to be believed. I remember walking with the Brigadier who had come to see what progress had been made; we were wading rather than walking in our wellington boots and the Brigadier said "Can't we get on to the road Padre?" I said "you're on the road Sir!" As soon as coke stoves were installed we all felt a lot happier and drier and warmer.

I feel I must record one incident that happened while we were still under canvas. The Battalion had been suffering from a fairly familiar complaint – gippy tummy. One night I was awakened by "Halt, who goes there?" Silence, except for the sound of running footsteps. A second "Halt, who goes there?" Silence. "Halt or I fire". Then followed a response which I hardly dare record here, but it indicated so succinctly, albeit so crudely, the marine's reason for having no intention of halting, that I feel it deserves a mention. "Halt be buggered, I'm shitting myself!" No shot was fired, the footsteps continued running and, hoping the man might reach his port of call in time, I turned over on my camp bed and giggled myself back to sleep.

I spent over a year on Woodbury Common, as Chaplain of 7th Battalion then of the 9th Battalion and eventually of the 8th Battalion which later became 41 Royal Marine Commando.

I was very nearly the cause of war between 9th and 8th Battalions, when I transferred from one unit to another. Our lines were so close that it struck me as sensible to get my MOA (Marine Officer's Attendant) to load up my wardrobe with all its drawers and contents in our 15cwt truck and run it over to my cabin in 8th Battalion lines, bringing the empty one back to the cabin I had occupied in 9th Battalion. I felt it would save a bit of packing and unpacking and the wardrobes were identical. I was aghast when the 9th Battalion Quartermaster visited me in some agitation to tell me I couldn't do such a thing. I managed to convince him of my ignorance as to why it was impossible and he explained that the necessary paperwork hadn't been done and that in any case no gear could be exchanged in such a casual manner with no official permission having been given. Fortunately Joe Barrett, QM 8th Battalion, was not only a more sensible type but he was friendly too and all was well. This friendship continued throughout the war and for many years after until Joe died in a home for old folk at Bembridge in the Isle of Wight. Joe had served for some incredibly long period in the Royal Marines and on retirement in the 1930s had become a porter at Christchurch, Oxford, but had been recalled at the outbreak of the 1939-45 war. He was a great asset to our 8th Battalion Officers' Mess and later to 41 Commando. He was a good companion, full of party tricks and could do anything with a pack of cards. Above all he was a good man and I was so happy when years after the war he wrote to tell me he had at last been confirmed. We had discussed this more than once but there had never been much chance of uninterrupted preparation.

In addition to a quarter of a Nissen hut as my cabin, a whole Nissen hut was allocated to the Chaplain to serve the dual purpose of Chapel and office.

It was used for services of Holy Communion and for discussion groups and it provided a place of quietness where men with problems could come to talk. Our Sunday morning services in the early days were held in the open air or under canvas. Life was quite pleasant on Woodbury Common during the summer of 1941 but with autumn and the approach of winter it became grim. The long walk of an evening down to Exmouth or Budleigh Salterton became less attractive. I was never quite sure if I was supposed to be entertainments officer but I got in touch with ENSA in Exeter and we managed to get one or two first class concert parties to the camp.

I also got hold of a large crate of indoor games but I can't remember how, or where they came from: dozens of packs of playing cards, dominoes, draughts, chess, ludo. It all helped to relieve the monotony and the misery of those dark damp winter nights.

Some time in the summer of 1942, we, 8th Battalion, were ordered to Llanion Barracks, Pembroke Docks. It was good after slumming it for 18 months in tents and Nissen Huts to enjoy what one could almost call the luxurious accommodation of a purpose built barracks, even though it wasn't exactly modern. I was provided with an office and there was a chapel as well, a fine recreation room and a NAAFI. We were all reasonably happy. We used to go off on two or three day exercises; the Prescelly hills were a favourite haunt and I remember getting somewhat irate because the practice grew up of beginning these exercises at 8am on a Sunday morning and then taking Thursday each week as the day off. I don't suppose it was anything to do with my protests but the practice was soon dropped. I associate these exercises and route marches with our CO at that time who had little or no sympathy with men suffering from badly blistered heels: they used to turn to the Chaplain for justice but all I could give them was sympathy. I was fortunate to be given a trip from Pembroke Dock to Mt. Batten in a Sunderland flying boat.

CHAPTER FOUR

With 41 Royal Marine Commando

After some months when we were happily settled in to barrack life we were told we were to become 41 Royal Marine Commando. This meant a certain amount of reorganisation: Companies were to become troops and every member of the unit had to be a volunteer and so we were able to lose all who weren't keen or weren't up to scratch. I was amazed to find that I was one of the oldest, only the CO and my MOA and one or two other men were older than I. Many years later I was invited to take a short memorial service at Royal Marines, Poole on 6th June, D. Day. As I walked into the Gymnasium and looked at the hundreds of marines in front of me I felt as if I were looking at a crowd of school boys, but then I realised that most of our men in 1942 had been between 18 and 20 years of age. We were transferred to Weymouth in Dorset and were very happy for the short time we spent there; it was a pleasant seaside resort with a cinema and all the amenities of a town. All members of the unit had to find their own accommodation; I and other H.Q. Troop Officers billeted ourselves in what was then the Burdon Hotel on the sea front opposite the pier entrance which was the troop parade ground. Each morning we could finish our breakfast coffee in comfort and make the parade in one minute flat. Apparently we were taken to Weymouth to rehearse with a Welsh Division a landing on a radar station a few miles round the coast which corresponded to a similar objective on the French coast. I gather it was one of Churchill's ideas for keeping the Germans on their toes. The whole exercise was such an unmitigated 'cock-up' that the idea was abandoned and our stay in Weymouth brought to a sudden end.

We were moved then to the Isle of Wight and the seven troops found themselves billets round the coast at Ryde, St Helens, Seaview and Bembridge. I had the job of knocking on doors and asking if they could put up a marine or two. It recalled the accommodating of London evacuee children in my parish in Wiltshire a year or so before. I suppose our stay in the Isle of Wight was for training in cliff climbing and for rehearsing dawn landings. I recall one very dirty night boarding a LCA at Ryde Pier and for an hour or so proceeding up Southampton Water and back being tossed about and made to feel very miserable; then back to make a landing in Osborne Bay. The young RNVR 2nd Lieutenants were obviously not as well up in navigation as they might have been and instead of landing us on a sloping sandy beach a number of the LCAs found themselves grounded on rocks 200 or 300 yards out from the shore.

This was at about 2am and in complete and utter darkness which added to the general panic, especially when the order was given for the unit to disembark. No one had any idea where we were, how deep the sea was or where the beach was and some men couldn't swim. There was nothing for it but for men to jump into the water with rifles held aloft. For a non-swimmer it was a grim prospect and it wasn't long before the order came to switch on the powerful flood lights on all the LCAs. It showed a scene of complete chaos: heads in helmets, arms, and rifles sticking up out of the water; LCAs balanced precariously on the rocks or tilted where some marines had jumped from the bows and left others still standing in the stern. It was this picture that gave me an idea: I thought that if I stood back and let others go ahead there might come a moment when the craft would regain its equilibrium and refloat. This is precisely what happened to the LCA I was in and I was eventually put on to the beach without even getting my feet wet. But there was one marine who was in a really bad way; he was a non-swimmer and had very nearly drowned before being pulled out of the water more dead than alive. He was strapped on to a stretcher and I and a corporal of marines went with him on a small craft to Ryde Pier. We managed to get him on his feet and we began the walk down the mile long pier, supporting him between us. About one quarter of the way along the pier he suddenly intimated in very crude terms that he needed urgently to answer a call of nature. We pulled his soaking wet trousers down at the double and squatted him

John (left) with 41 Marine Commando Sergeants (centre) Alec Dunn and (right) Jack Tanswell at Deal in 1944. Both sergeants served with 'B' Troop in the original unit which was formed in October of 1942.

in the middle of the pier and all the trauma and shock of the night passed through him. On more than one occasion since I have walked past that spot when the pier has been full of trippers and holidaymakers and have thought of that marine. We took him to Ryde hospital and he was eventually invalided out of the Service.

After one of these night landings we were crowded into a large nissen hut and were privileged to meet the Chief of Combined Operations, Lord Louis Mountbatten. His brief talk and his charisma captured us all and one felt that everyone there was willing to follow him unquestioningly.

These night exercises usually ended in our having to hang around for hours once we were ashore in the mud and in all sorts of weather. Just before Christmas I picked up a chill and I suppose because we were living in a hotel, the MO thought it would be better for all concerned if I was transferred to the small Naval sick bay at Seaview. I enjoyed my stay there but for some reason I was taken to the Royal Naval

27

hospital at Haslar on the mainland where I was to spend more time many years later.

I have not said much about my work as Chaplain apart from providing Sunday morning worship and occasional services of Holy Communion when we were in camp and in barracks but from the time we became a Commando unit and our men lived in digs over a wide area, with no Chaplain's office and with no Chapel it became even more difficult to arrange Sunday worship and do the traditional work of a Chaplain.

One made oneself available as Counsellor to those with problems and most of these were marital and domestic and one accepted the job of Welfare Officer. It was really a matter of being with the unit, of being friendly to all and approachable. I feel sure this is where the wisdom of the Royal Navy helps, by giving a Chaplain no rank. I had the opportunity and I think I could say it was a privilege of sharing life with the unit in all their exercises, route marches, blisters, weariness, soakings, sleeping rough and bivouacing in extremely low temperatures, and sharing in the fun too.

Perhaps one of the most useful jobs I did while we were in the Isle of Wight and in Scotland, and one that helped me to keep in touch with the seven troops of the Commando when we were scattered over a wide area was to go to each troop and get their orders for tobacco, cigarettes, chocolate etc. from NAAFI. Then collecting the goods from the nearest NAAFI and taking them round to the HQ office of the seven troops at a scheduled time when the customers would be awaiting. I enjoyed this; it was fun and it was appreciated.

It was while we were in the Isle of Wight that a couple of troops at a time were sent to a street-fighting school at East Ham. I asked to go with the first batch. We were billeted in workmen's flats, with running water and electric light but not much more in the way of domestic comfort. We had our own camp beds and blankets and breakfast was provided.

We were all shattered to see the devastation of the East End: there weren't many houses left intact in the areas we were exercising in. One of the earlier exercises was to face-up to flame throwers. We were put into what was left of the front room of houses and then a flame throwing machine would slowly make its way down the road pouring great floods of flame through what had originally been windows. We were crouched against the wall under the window, wrapped in a blanket.

The terror of seeing this wall of flame coming straight for us, and not any damage it did to us or to the house was all that could be said in favour of flame throwers.

The more exciting part of the street fighting school was the Assault course. We had all had a taste of assault courses in our training, but this was a bigger and better one than we'd ever experienced before. It was a regular daily performance. To begin with I found it nearly killed me, not because I wasn't fit, but because so much of it was so very difficult and the whole thing was made more off-putting because of the liberal use of thunder flashes and of live ammunition.

Gradually one began to get the hang of things and by the end of the first week I felt less frightened of the course and more able to cope. So much so that when the first two troops went back to the Isle of Wight I asked if I could be allowed to stay at East Ham for the following two weeks until our unit had done the street fighting course.

Needless to say having had a week's start on the two fresh troops the Padre's performance on the Assault Course sent his shares up considerably and by the 3rd week the course presented little difficulty to him and his agility earned him quite a bit of respect. I must confess this was not the only object of my wanting to spend 3 weeks in the East End. We always returned to the workmen's flats by 5pm and enjoyed a good wash down from all the dirt and rubble we inevitably picked up on and under our denims. Then a change into KSD and off to the West End for a meal and perhaps a Show.

Eventually we all returned to the Isle of Wight.

We enjoyed our time in the Isle of Wight. No visitors were allowed on the Island. Food and drink were plentiful and the Hotel in which I and the HQ troop officers were billeted had pre-war stocks of wine. We were sad to have to pack up and entrain to Scotland and we ended up in Ayrshire. I think the Heads of Ayr were the challenge for our climbers. There was a fleet of flat bottomed landing craft at Troon and the Isle of Arran was available for our night landings. I and my fellow officers in HQ troop were very comfortably housed and fed and looked after by Mistress Hendry in a guest house, Mar Lodge. She treated us as an old but rather sweet clucking hen would treat her chicks. After lots of dawn landings, a good deal of sea sickness and lots of soakings I suppose we all became more able to cope with whatever our future held in store. One day the unit was rushed over to Greenock to board ship and we all thought "This is it" but within an hour we were disembarked and ordered to return to Troon.

CHAPTER FIVE

The Landing in Sicily

At last in the summer of 1943 after two years training we boarded SS *Durban Castle* in the Clyde and we knew this time that we were on the way. The ship was rigged with 22 LCAs, flat bottomed landing craft, holding 35 men each. We sailed down the Clyde in a fairly large convoy containing a Canadian division. Needless to say we had no idea where we were going, security was good but obviously the fact that we had been kitted out with bush shirts and shorts indicated we were going south. It was some days before we were informed of our destination and each day after that we had to spend time studying maps and models and the particular bit of coastline in South East Sicily where we were to silence the coastal guns and lead the Canadian troops ashore.

It was while we were passing through the Bay of Biscay that we had our first experience of war at sea. It was the most glorious summer's evening, the sun had not yet set and the sea was as calm as the proverbial millpond. Suddenly action stations sounded and we were told that the convoy was about to be attacked by U boats. The ship to the stern of us carrying a Canadian Field Ambulance unit was torpedoed. We felt the loss of this ship a month or two later at Salerno.

I had a roving commission as far as action stations were concerned and I felt my place was with the men on their mess decks which on this large liner were 5 decks down. I can still hear those depth charges exploding, sounding as if they were about to tear the bottom of the Durban Castle to pieces as the destroyers fired off their patterns. We soon got organised on the most popular pastime, apart from tombola, or bingo as it is called today, that of the general knowledge quiz. Its popularity was due not to a desire for knowledge, but more to the competitive side of it: troop against troop, mess against mess. We spent many hours at it in all sorts of places. It certainly took our minds off the unpleasantness of torpedoes and of the frightening sound of depth charges. At length the all clear was sounded and we were released from the bowels of the ship.

On the Sunday before the landing was due to take place a service of Holy Communion was held in one of the ship's public rooms and a goodly number of men attended; it was as if they understood it was a service of dedication to the cause in hand. The convoy slipped through the Straits of Gibraltar by midnight without mishaps and the next never-to-be-forgotten sight was the converging of all the convoys, one from Alexandria, one from Malta and our own from the Clyde, on the afternoon of the day before our landings. Most of us had never before seen so many ships together. We were to synchronize our watches at 1600 hours when the ball dropped from the masthead of Admiral Vian's flagship. A tremendous gale was blowing and a heavy sea running and the odds against the landings going ahead were considerable, but at 4pm down came the ball from the top of the mast. All we could do now was to wait patiently and prepare for the landing. We had practised our boat stations so many times in daylight and in complete darkness that we could quite easily and quickly find our way from our cabins or mess decks to our boat stations. At about 10pm we were given our last meal aboard, a very large and satisfying dinner. One extraordinary thing is worth mentioning here: a certain Lieutenant RM who normally had the appetite of a horse sat at the table looking exceedingly pale and unable to face his food and all our coaxing couldn't change his mind. Within five hours he was dead, shot as he ran up the beach.

I was not allowed to land in the first flight which left the ship at about 12.30am so I was able to watch from the rail of the Durban Castle all the landing craft load up. It was by no means easy because at one moment one end of the LCA was level with the gangway platform and the next moment it was 4 or 5 feet lower, so great was the swell. We lay about 7 miles off the coast; it was pitch black and the channel to the beach had been marked by a series of floating red lights. One of the landing craft had trouble with its engine and

32

had to return to the Durban Castle; the 35 marines aboard were not amused. I was tremendously impressed by the display put up by the RAF and by the two RN monitors, I think it was HMS *Erebus* and HMS *Roberts*, bombarding Pachino on the South Eastern tip of Sicily. Eventually the second flight was ordered away; it was just beginning to get less dark and I remember glimpsing in the distance the tops of the hills standing out above the dense early morning mist.

I found that getting aboard the landing craft was not easy because, in addition to full embarkation order, a heavy back pack, a side pack and a Red Cross pack, I had, round my waist, ten tins containing 50 Woodbines apiece as well as my Mae West. Judging the moment to jump onto the rather confined space on the LCA was not easy but at length I was seated with the 34 other passengers, unable to move forward or backward or from side to side. A good description would have been "packed like sardines". It wasn't long before the heavy swell took its toll and the only place to be sick was down the back of the chap in front and I think most of the fellows were sick, but for some reason I wasn't. It was a nightmare trip; its one saving feature was that when our time came to land and run up the beach we were past caring if we were shot. The beach heaved and fell for some time after we got ashore, almost as terrifyingly as the LCA.

The landing was not as straightforward as it might have been because there were a series of false bottoms and eventually our craft stuck about 200 yards off shore in water about 4 feet deep. We had to jump for it. My MOA was a very short man and he was scared that if he should happen to fall backwards when he jumped he would never be able to get upright again but would inevitably drown. With back and side pack, rifle and sundry other bits and pieces I could see his point and I assured him I would be right behind him and I guaranteed his safety. I wasn't feeling altogether free and easy myself with those tins of Woodbines each suspended by string from a bit of rope round my middle and with the inflated Mae West which didn't add to one's freedom of movement. Needless to say the Mae Wests were the first bit of gear we dispensed with as soon as we waded up the beach.

I tried to maintain my identity as Chaplain while we were

33

in action in Sicily and Italy by wearing a dog-collar even though they were merely white cardboard ones which would become off-white and very limp with sweat. I also wore a red cross armlet. My first aid pack proved indispensable: shell dressings, small bandages, a bottle of morphia, sulphanilamide powder and scissors. My side pack contained the usual necessities: tooth brush, shaving brush, razor, soap, small towel etc. It also contained four items more important than all these: a prayer book and a bible, without which no priest could maintain his duty of saying the daily offices of matins and evensong, and a pack of cards and a cribbage board. I'm tempted to say I don't know which proved the more useful.

Having discarded our Mae Wests we made for the low bank at the top of the beach. Where we landed that bank couldn't have been more than 3-3$\frac{1}{2}$ feet high and I found no difficulty in clambering up it. The unit landed on various parts of the beaches in that South Eastern tip of Sicily and in places the cliff, if you could call it that, might have been as much as 12 feet high.

The unit had been sent to Scotland in order to train on scaling the Heads of Ayr because reconnaissance planes coming in at sea level to these Sicilian beaches and then suddenly climbing up and away steeply had produced photographs of almost unscaleable cliffs. My batman and I started off round the coast to try to link up with the main body of the unit. I was intrigued with a number of what looked to be white pools or lakes a mile or two ahead of us. They turned out to be salt pits. The next thing that caught our eye was the barrel of a 25 pounder sticking up out of the water and not much further on a dead Canadian Sergeant on the sand, facing inland with a clean wound in his back. I think he must have been one of the more unpopular Sergeants in that unit. After walking for some time along the pathway at the top of the sandy beach we came across the first dead marine. Someone had covered him with his gas cape and when I pulled it off I was somewhat shaken to find what a mess he was in and how black his flesh and blood were. He had been lying there since sunrise and by midday the sun was burning hot. Not many yards from him was an Italian pill-box with 3 or 4 dead Italians lying in and

34

around the entrance. Apparently our marines had surprised the inmates of the pill-box and ordered them out with hands up. One of the Italians at the rear had lobbed a plastic grenade and this was the cause of the bloody state of the dead marine. No Italian came out of that pill-box alive. It was difficult to know what to do about burying the dead because there was little or no top soil, it was mostly rock; the vines seemed to do quite well on it! We managed to get together a small burial party of Italians our fellows had taken prisoner and they dug graves as best they could. A Corporal of marines with his rifle was in charge but for some reason he disappeared round the corner of a stone wall just as one of the Italians pulled out of the pocket of one of the corpses a plastic grenade. He had already relieved the dead of the rings they were wearing: that didn't worry me but I was scared to see that grenade, especially when he looked at me. With what I realised afterwards was great presence of mind I held out my hand and shouted "Da me" which I thought meant "give it to me" and was about all the Italian I knew. He did and I presented it to the Corporal when he reappeared.

My next set of burials that day left me with an uneasy conscience. Five men had been mown down on the beach. At the top of that beach away from the water line the sea weed was many feet thick. I took the line of least resistance and we dug holes in the sea weed and buried the dead. I thought that as there were no tides in the Mediterranean it should be all right, and in addition to this we had to give a map reference for every burial, and I knew the War Graves Commission would soon find them. After these burials on the first morning ashore I came to the unit's casualty clearing station where there were ten or a dozen of our fellows lying on camp beds or palliasses. On one of them was our Adjutant lying on his tummy. He twisted his head round and looked up at me with a mischievous smile and said "I've been shot in the arse Padre". He hadn't kept it down low enough crawling under the barbed wire defences. Another officer, a Troop Commander, was being sick into his helmet; he had been quite badly wounded in the shoulder. Sitting around outside were a few SBAs, (Sick Berth Attendants), and some marines. I joined them and was glad to sit down and have a bit of a rest. Suddenly there was a sharp crack of a rifle shot and a marine fell forward. We all flattened ourselves on the ground assuming there was a sniper in the locality. Then a man who had been cleaning his rifle said "Gawd, there must have been one up the spout". We ripped the shirt off the man who had been shot and it was obvious nothing could be done for him. The bullet had entered his chest and come out of his back; he was dead. As the afternoon wore on I began to feel very tired and hungry and the heat was intense. We had landed at around 3-4am and we had had no sleep before that. I decided to make my way round the coast to where I understood Brigade HQ to be to try and get a meal and to find somewhere to get my head down for the night.

Almost immediately on arrival I was asked by the Brigadier to get hold of a mule cart and with the Brigade Major to oversee the evacuation from the casualty clearing station before nightfall of our remaining wounded. The stretchers were loaded up. The sun had set and the light was failing. We set off back to HQ. Quite suddenly the Brigade Major flung an arm across me holding me back and hissed "Get down, Padre!" and we both fell flat on our tummies. He pulled out his revolver. There to the right of our path was a row of kneeling Italians or Germans, in fact it looked as if there was more than one row. I thought "this is it" and the heart pounded away to such an extent that I thought my lungs would burst. Then there came a snigger from the Brigade Major as he got up, putting his revolver back into its holster. This gave me the courage to peer through the dusk at the enemy: rows of vines about $3^1/_2$ feet high. I was reminded of some lines from Shakespeare talking of "strong imagination" in Midsummer Nights Dream which I once had to study as a set book.

> "In the night imagining some fear,
> How easy is a bush supposed a bear".

On arriving back at Brigade HQ my MOA who was a gem, found a tin of self-heating soup which just about saved my life. Followed by a tin of date pudding. I slept exceedingly well that night although it was on the stone floor of a stable, with two black Americans and lots of mosquitos. I smothered my face and neck with anti-mosquito cream but I think the mosquitos had very little understanding of what the cream was for, so I wasn't too upset when I found my tin of cream missing the next morning. My MOA produced a bucket of hot water from somewhere and I was able to wash and shave before tucking into a huge plateful of porridge with a couple of cups of steaming tea.

One of our marines killed on the beach on that first day was a cockney lad, always full of fun, and a great loss to the unit. The initial landing was timed for 0350 hours. Many months later when I spent a couple of weeks visiting as many of the next-of-kin of our casualties as possible I had a most interesting talk to the mother and father of this man. Apparently he had as a pet an Airedale dog: the two of them were inseparable. On the night of the 10th July 1943 the dog was put to bed in its basket as usual and the old folk went up to bed. The dog didn't settle and its whimpering kept them awake. The father came downstairs and warmed some milk, thinking the dog was uncomfortable and that this might soothe it. It didn't and for an hour or two it became more and more agitated, whimpering and crying until at about 4am it suddenly became quite quiet. When the old chap went down to see what had happened he found the dog dead.

CHAPTER SIX

In Sicily

We settled in for a few days on a site not far from the beaches where we landed. It was rumoured that a sniper was around and a farm house not far inland was thought to be his hideout; a raid was organised one night and unfortunately one of our marines was shot. No one knew if it was a mistake on the part of one of our men, or an accident, or the lack of a challenge and a password. No sniper was found.

It was either on the second or third night ashore that my MOA and I found a very nice little bungalow with just one living room with a beautifully cool tiled mosaic floor to lie on. Round the walls were piles of maize and beans and vegetables of all kinds. We had been warned not to drink from the wells because the water might have been polluted, but we found at the back of this bungalow a huge tank of wine, nicely chilled. My training as a priest had taught me a fair amount about self-control but how could one sleep, with an unquenchable thirst, knowing that just outside was a tank of wine? My enamel mug held just a pint; I purposely didn't fill it but I had enough to quench my thirst. After an hour or so I found sleep didn't come easily because I was still thirsty and my mind kept turning to that tank of lovely wine. So again I took my mug, put it under the tap and gave myself the other half. I shall always remember the utter bliss of that Sicilian plonk. There was an unfortunate ending to the story. One of our marines apparently couldn't stop visiting the tank. The next morning 2 or 3 marines were needed to hold him down and get him into a small Fiat which was all we could lay our hands on to get him into hospital: he was in a bad way.

When we had more or less settled in to our new surroundings I felt it would be right to suggest that we had a short service followed by Holy Communion. That Holy Communion Service has left an indelible impression.

I have conducted and attended many communion services in parish churches, in College chapels, in tents, in the open air, on board ship but never anything quite like that one. I had no table or box or anything that could be used as an altar but appropriately enough a nearby Sicilian farmhouse had a well standing outside its door, and its stone wall was just the right height. A clean handkerchief made a "fair linen cloth" which the Prayer Book prescribes. I had lost all my Chaplain's gear in our landing so I used my tin mug as a chalice. I asked the farmer's wife if she could let me have some bread and a little wine. The bread was bean bread, as hard as ship's biscuits but I managed to chip pieces off it. The wine was the Sicilian plonk.

We held the service before sunset because dusk creeps up on one fairly quickly. It was a perfect evening, the sky was full of crimson and yellows as the sun began sinking. It was utterly peaceful, out of this world. Between 20 and 30 men attended. Kneeling in a wide circle round the well, one felt a sense of reality about the attendance of these men at this service rather different from Church Parades or camp and barrack services. They were thankful for the fact that they were alive and well when some of their pals had been killed or wounded. I also shared their sense of gratitude towards those who were killed. It was almost a feeling that they had died so that we might survive and that we owed them a debt of gratitude. The feeling remained real with me for many years especially after our heavy casualties at Salerno and each time I celebrated Holy Communion I remembered them. I became reconciled to the hymn, so popular with the Royal British legion, 'O Valiant hearts', the words of which some people consider heretical, if not blasphemous, and which before the war I thought a bit far-fetched when it spoke of "lesser cavalries".

Although we lost our gear when we landed, except what we carried ashore with us, we seemed to manage perfectly well. The essentials like a clean bush shirt and a pair of socks were in our back packs. I regretted the loss of a rather fine silver communion set presented to me when I left the Wiltshire parish where I had served as curate; I had packed it securely in an ammunition box with RN hymn cards and other bits and pieces for use at services. Some time later when I was serving in the Home Fleet at Scapa Flow a large parcel arrived for me: a biscuit tin containing this Communion Set. A letter from the Chaplain of the Fleet explained that it had been found on the steps of the Italian naval base in Augusta, Sicily. It was passed to the Royal Naval Chaplain there and he had forwarded it to the Chaplain of the Fleet who had sent it up to Scapa Flow. Fortunately it had an engraving on the bottom of the paten: "Presented to the Reverend John Wallis...."

Some days after our landing and before we had moved any further I was told that a marine was lying dead and unburied in a vineyard. I was given a map reference and instructions as to where I should find him. I managed to get some transport and with one or two helpers we set off. One of the reasons why his friends were keen that we should find him was because they knew that he had taken £18 ashore with him which was a lot of money in 1943 and it seemed a pity not to try to recover it. We found him: we couldn't miss him lying face downward, he was the size of a pony, swollen up beyond belief with his shirt and shorts almost at bursting point. He had no boots on. Some Sicilian had the finest pair of boots he was ever likely to own. It was quite impossible to touch him and so he was the one and only man I buried whose identity disc I did not remove. The cord was buried deeply in the swollen folds of the flesh of his neck. Each man wore two discs, one was removed when a person was buried and one was left on for identification purposes by the War Graves Commission. Strange things can happen: one day a marine brought me an identity disc he had picked up in the ablution centre belonging to a man I had buried months before.

After some days the unit moved up the coast road through Syracuse towards Augusta and one saw something of the devastation caused by the bombardment on the South East tip of Sicily by the RN Monitors on the night of our landing. Even so the beauty of the white houses, the blue of the sea, and the gloriously coloured flowering trees and shrubs along the sides of the roads seemed to make up for the ugliness of the destruction.

I was fortunate in being provided with a 500cc Triumph motorcycle but in spite of wearing goggles I had to stop frequently to clean them and both I and my motorcycle were coated in the very fine chalk dust which lay to a depth of some inches on every road. For a short while we were dug in in olive groves outside the village of Brucoli. We had to dig slit trenches because early each morning an Italian plane came sweeping along the olive grove, machine gunning. I suppose they must have known we were there although we tried to keep out of sight, especially when a plane was heard. We were never hit, but it was a nuisance. We were short of water and this hit our washing of ourselves and our shirts. A biscuit tin of water had to do for 4 or 5 of us to wash and shave. We managed to get to the sea for a swim in the early evening but if people think our seas and rivers are polluted in England today, they should have seen what floated in Sicilian waters.

One evening we were caught by an Italian plane which was strafing a Royal Naval vessel two or three hundred yards off the coast where we were swimming. We felt safe as long as we were in the water but we felt it would be tempting providence to clamber up on the rocks to collect our shorts.

The track down to this bathing place led through a primitive little hamlet and one day, because I was wearing the Red Cross armband, I was asked to have a look at one or two wounded Sicilians who were in what had obviously been their sick bay or first aid post. It was just a cave in the hillside and was very unpleasant indeed with filthy straw and bloody rags. I was asked if I would bury one of their casualties. He lay in a field some way out of the village and he must have been there since the initial landings a week or more before.

I was surprised how quickly one came to recognise the smell of death and in those early weeks in Sicily I associated it with Cypress trees, I suppose because I happened on more than one occasion to find either our own or enemy dead nearby. The stench on this occasion was so bad that we had to wear gas masks before we could get near enough to start burying. It took 2 or 3 marines some time to dig the grave in the rocky soil and with their gas masks on they very nearly passed out with heat exhaustion. Then came the most horrible part of the proceedings. The corpse was lying face downwards; when we turned him over there was no chest left, just a seething mass of maggots. We shovelled him into the grave as best we could.

Italian planes were still raiding our shipping and gun emplacements especially at night, and one, a Focke Wolfe as we discovered the next day, came zooming down in flames over a cemetery full of marble tombs and monuments and I couldn't help wondering what damage it was about to do. We were lying up along a stone wall which surrounded the cemetery. It was a terrifying sight as the blazing plane screamed over our heads but it hit the ground well outside the cemetery.

The guns around the harbour of Augusta were manned by the MNBDO. The Marine Naval Base Defence Organisation and we knew a number of their officers, the home of one of them was three doors away from my digs in Trowbridge, Wiltshire. We used to watch their searchlight display each night and listen to their guns. One night we heard a strange whine which increased until it ended in a dull thud close to where we were standing. It turned out to be dud shell. Everyone marched smartly away.

One morning our Mess Corporal and several MOAs who had been collecting stores from the base at Augusta asked if I would come and bury an Italian airman they had found in the sea as they had been scrambling over the rocks. They had dragged him ashore but there was no chance of burying him properly; all we could do was to cover him with small rocks and stones, mark the spot with a cairn and fill in a burial form giving a map reference. He was not a pretty sight; he had a head but no face

CHAPTER SEVEN

Last Days in Sicily

Water was a problem, particularly drinking water. Warned that the wells may have been polluted, Sicilian plonk was very welcome. Another Sicilian product was water melons, once we found ourselves near a field full of ripe red melons as large as pumpkins. This was one of the few occasions on which I used my issue Commando knife, which I wore tucked down my stocking.

We sliced the melon in half, scooped out the pips and then buried our faces in it. Some of us were a bit wary of eating too many and we were cautious of tomatoes thinking of Malta Fever or dysentery. Actually dysentery didn't take long to strike and many of us were soon on the run: the vine didn't help. It was a debilitating business and it seemed to take all the energy and sparkle out of life and if it continued for any length of time one began to feel really depressed.

The MO eventually arranged for me to go into an Italian hospital. It was a joy to sleep in a bed with sheets and to have a bath and decent food, but the dysentery continued to spoil all this. At last I was given a dose of something connected with poppies and I slept for 36 hours non-stop and on waking I found the plague had ceased.

After a week or so we left our olive groves on the outskirts of Augusta and travelled up the coast road to lemon groves outside Catania. We were glad to get into a town of some size with decent shops. The barbers' establishments seemed to be as popular as pubs in England and we all began to smell very sweet. The Prince Borghese had a superior residence in Catania, I suppose it could be called a Palace, and some of us enjoyed a visit and a browse among the books in his library which included a number of English books. While in Catania we made an attempt to climb Mount Etna. We didn't start until the afternoon and I for one still felt too weak from dysentery to hope to reach the summit.

On the way down it was good to see the lights of the town beneath us. Darkness fell very quickly after sunset and there was no blackout. It was the first time we had seen such a sight for some years.

One lunchtime we in HQ troop were just about to sit down to our bully and biscuits when there was the most almighty explosion. It seemed to come from the railway line which ran to Catania along the coast from Messina. We piled into whatever transport we could find and dashed off down the road in the direction of the explosion. A railway truck loaded with ammunition of all kinds had blown up and there was nothing left. I was told that one or two men from an Army Regiment had been blown up with it. All we found were a few bits and pieces stuck to the rocky outcrop alongside the railway line. We collected what fragments we could in a sack and I gave them Christian burial. One didn't feel much like lunch after that episode.

I think this was the place and the time that I received my one and only war wound. The Quarter Master Sergeant had just opened a large tin of Woodbines about the size of a biscuit tin. He had opened three sides with a tin opener and had bent back the jagged lid. I unfortunately walked into it and the jagged edge cut my calf quite deeply. For weeks, the flies, which were always everywhere wouldn't leave it alone and it became septic and it was months before it eventually healed and it left me with a scar. If and when anyone asks "what's that?" I airily reply "I picked that up in Sicily".

One day I was asked to act as King's Messenger to take some dispatches to Palermo. I boarded a plane at Catania airfield which had been badly bombed by the Allies before the Germans had been cleared out. It was a short but interesting trip over the fields and farms and vineyards and hills and villages and the plane flew at a low altitude which gave me the chance to pick out details, especially of the hill top villages we passed over.

I found the mixture of Norman and Moorish architecture in Palermo and other towns of Sicily most attractive. It was not long after this that the unit was ordered to pack up and report to Milazzo on the north coast to board ship to make another landing. This entailed a trip in a jeep covering a good deal of the same country I had so recently flown over.

CHAPTER EIGHT

Touch and Go at Salerno

It was good to get on a ship again and to enjoy the food provided. On the first evening aboard after supper I was playing a game of crib with one of the engineer officers when suddenly and unexpectedly there was a tremendous explosion. We rocked considerably but didn't sink so we concluded we had not been hit but on going up on deck we saw a large gaping hole in the side of the LCT nearest to us. Obviously a mine had floated into the harbour; we wondered if there were any more around. We sailed without much more delay thinking we were probably to make our landing at Naples. Then we heard over the radio that Italy had capitulated and we all concluded we were in for a jolly weekend in Naples. Little did we know what awaited us.

The main objective of Operation Avalanche, as it was called, carried out by the British 10th Corps and the American 6th Corps was the capture of Naples. Our first objective was the town of Vietri.

Again I was not allowed to land in the first flight but went in with the transport section. We thought it strange to be greeted with so much gun fire as we approached the shore and we did not feel at all happy when the sand began to fly around us as we drove off the landing craft on to the beach. Mortar bombs were landing too frequently and too close for our liking. The Italians may have given in but the Germans certainly had not.

There was one building that stood out distinctly as we approached the shore: a tobacco factory and as a pipe smoker I found it interesting to take a closer look at it once we had landed. I passed a dead German but was taking no chances of burying him in case he was booby-trapped. We set off in convoy along the coast road to Salerno but had not gone very far before we were pulled up suddenly and we could see tanks, trucks, and jeeps stretching away ahead of us. We waited and waited and nothing moved. At last the transport Sergeant with whom I was travelling got out of the jeep and walked along to the head of the queue. He came running back with several other drivers who had gone to find out the cause of the delay. Apparently there was a German 88mm just round the corner.

Everyone got into reverse and there was a fair amount of chaos. We ended up by leaving our transport and finding a temporary residence in a deep ditch which fortunately at that time of year was bone dry. After the rains it no doubt became a small river. We spent the next few days and nights in this ditch; by "we" I mean the transport section of 41 Commando. The rest of the unit had landed on the north side of Salerno and we were eager to get through to them.

We found we were sharing the ditch with all sorts of bits of units, there were South Africans and New Zealanders with us. We daren't attempt to move because a German plane had a nasty habit of flying along the ditch machine gunning. As far as I know he never hit anyone, but he did keep us pinned down. At length we got on the move again and made for the town of Salerno along the open coast road which was under fire from German guns and mortars. At regular intervals huge notices advised us that if we wished to keep our heads we should keep our distance.

All seemed quiet when we arrived in Salerno. We drove through the town to Vieri Sul Mare where we linked up with the rest of the unit. Their job had been to take the large naval guns: they looked like 16 inch guns, set in the hill side. It was a pleasant little coastal village.

Three of us, a troop commander, the Signals officer and myself took over a small cottage, or rather the one bed-room, where I slept on the bed and the other two on the floor. The Padre was given a certain amount of respect!

We were a bit worried at the amount of mortar fire but we put our trust in the Lord and went to sleep. It was the most comfortable night I'd spent for some time.

The next morning it was Sunday I remember, and our troubles started. We were ordered to guard the road to Naples which was under attack by the Germans. It meant crossing a large torrent bed by a viaduct which was visible to the enemy and therefore under fire. We commandeered a bungalow as a field dressing station and it wasn't long before our casualties began arriving and all that day the MO and the sick berth attendants and I were doing our best to dress the wounds and to make as comfortable as possible the dozens of men – army types as well as our own RM Commandos – before loading them up on ambulances to be taken to hospital. It meant that the ambulance had to cross that bridge and this meant that at a certain point both the driver, but more especially the helper sitting on his left, had to get their heads right down in order not to present a Gerry sniper with a target. I did the trip once and I must confess it was a great relief to reach the cover offered by the houses at the end of the bridge.

It was swelteringly hot in that Italian bungalow and although the main room or hall was quite large, half a dozen stretcher cases and 3 or 4 helpers made it a bit of a crush and men had to be patched up as quickly as possible and laid outside to await the next ambulance.

On more than one occasion when dressing their wounds I found some lines from Geoffrey Studdert Kennedy about the wounded, from his verse, 'Solomon in all his glory', running through my head:

'Purple robes and snowy linen
Have for earthly kings sufficed,
But these bloody, sweaty tatters
Were the robes of Jesus Christ.'

Other memories that stand out clearly: the frightening amount of blood about the place, the colossal number of Woodbine cigarettes that were smoked both by wounded and MO and Padre and the SBAs. My worst memory is of a Lieutenant in an army regiment who was brought in screaming and writhing with pain. We couldn't get anything out of him as to where he was hurt and we couldn't find any trace of a wound. I remember injecting almost all the morphia I had left in the bottle in my First Aid Kit but it did no good. He was eventually taken off by ambulance. After three days the unit had lost 12 killed, 74 wounded and 67 missing.

Our heavyweight boxer was brought in having had both

cheeks of his bottom sliced off by shrapnel. There was a good deal of blood about but he didn't seem unduly perturbed. He was a big man and I used a tremendous amount of sulphanilamide powder on him; this was the latest drug used on every wound.

Some months later on a railway station back in England – it was either Wrexham or Crewe – I came across this man with others of our unit who had been wounded at Salerno. They all seemed to be in good form and were being transferred to a convalescent depot: it was quite a reunion.

Another memory stands out of that particular period at Salerno. For some reason I had gone up one evening to the Naples road, I suppose to see some of our men and I recall going into a large barn; a fire was burning in the barn and the place was very smokey indeed. An army chaplain was trying to sort out the bits and pieces of casualties which one tried to package up to be sent home to the next-of-kin. Whether it was the smokey atmosphere making his eyes water or the grieving for his dead comrades, or whether he was inexperienced or was fearful getting near the end of his tether I don't know, but I knew how he felt and tried to encourage him.

Some time later, it may have been days or it may have been a week or more, we were taken in trucks to a new area NE of Salerno where the Germans were exerting a good deal of pressure. There was a Hermann Goering Panzer unit facing us and it seemed as if we were very short of tanks. I remember seeing two of our tanks crippled at a bridge which had been demolished. We were alongside No.2 Army Commando in which Captain the Duke of Wellington served. He was killed leading a charge against a German machine gun post. I saw his helmet. It was holed in 3 or 4 places. His grave was close to one of our sick berth attendants whom I buried, whose name was Horace Garlick. He came from the East End of London. He was killed trying to bring in one of our badly wounded marines. I've often felt that the words of Ecclesiasticus apply so aptly to these two men:

to the Duke of Wellington:
Let us now praise famous men
Men renowned for their power

Leaders of the people, rich men furnished
with ability
Honoured in their generation
There be of them that have left a name
behind them.

to Horace Garlick:
And some there be which have no memorial
Who are perished as though they had never been
But these were merciful men, whose
righteousness hath not been forgotten
Their glory shall not be blotted out.

The terraced slopes of these hills among which we found
ourselves were very beautiful at that time of the year: the
time of the grape harvest. One felt sorry for the owners of
the vineyards because there was little hope of their gathering a harvest in 1943. Some of the hillsides reminded one
of pictures of Flanders in the 1914-18 War: just the bare
trunks of trees which had been hacked about by shell fire
and mortar bombs.

It was at night that one was able to get on with burying
the dead. Daylight was dangerous because the German lines
were no distance away and even at night one was all the
time apprehensive. It was a sheer sense of duty and no brav-
ery or courage, that moved me to go in search of the dead.
Usually I was given some idea of where to find casualties. I
found that men were very concerned about their dead
friends being given proper burial, and on more than one
occasion I had argued that it was better to leave one's mate
out in the open, in what one might call "no-mans-land" than
risk being shot in the attempt to get him back to our lines.
I reckoned it was all right to risk one's life for a wounded
man but not for a dead man.

It was difficult if there was no moonlight although one
didn't want too much of it. You certainly couldn't shine a
torch to find your way up the hillside tracks, but as I say I
was usually accompanied by a friend of the dead man who
knew exactly where we had to go. I was taken aback one
night by finding a completely naked white body, standing out
quite sharply in the gloom. All he had on was his boots and

the feet of his socks in the boots. It was on the same night that I had one of the most difficult burials in my life. The man was lying with his arms outstretched. He was a very large fellow and even to cover his body with the rocky soil of the terraced vineyard was going to be a long job, but his limbs were so stiff that there was no question of folding them into his body. I had the Intelligence Officer with me and a Corporal who knew where the casualties were. We did our best, working as quietly as we could with the entrenching tools because we knew we must be very close to the German lines. We daren't stand up and so we had to work on our knees crouched as low as possible in the moonlight. I happened to look up over the stone terrace and there where the ground dropped away to the next terrace, in the gloom I saw a German helmet just a few yards away gently moving forward towards us. The Intelligence Officer pulled his revolver and I tried to bury myself where we had been scratching the soil wondering who would fire first. A laugh relieved the tension. The cause of the panic was a large low vine leaf swaying in the pale moonlight almost indistinguishable in shape from a German helmet.

I was glad that I knew most of the relevant parts of the Burial Office by heart because almost all the burials were at night. One had to fill up a burial return, giving full details and a map reference. Then one had to find some way of marking the grave, sometimes with a simple cross made of sticks, if any were available, or with the man's helmet and this applied to any Germans buried, if details were available.

I had more than one of these frightening experiences! One night I must have been out between our lines and the Germans, without knowing it, because on returning down the hillside I turned a corner of a terrace and there were two or three men lying flat on their tummies with rifles pointing at me. I felt sure they were Germans until I heard one of them say "cornflakes" and I immediately came out with "custard". It was essential to remember the nightly password.

On another night on the way up a hill to bury the dead I came across the RSM – the Regimental Sergeant Major. It must have been about 1am and I thought he seemed somewhat distraught and not his usual self. That was the last night that he was seen and no remains, no trace of him at all was ever found. We had other instances of this complete disappearance and one can only assume a direct hit from shell or mortar bomb. It was most unsatisfactory, and disturbing for the next of kin and I received letters from a mother, a widow and a father, who obviously wanted to know more about the date and circumstances of a death.

I think the real "low" of the whole war, as far as I was concerned, was when I was asked early one morning to go up to a point on a hillside where I had spent a pleasant hour or two the previous afternoon, playing crib and chatting and brewing up. When I came to the spot I could scarcely believe my eyes: the same 5 or 6 marines were in much the same positions as they had been when I left them the afternoon before, but they were all dead. I had an uncanny feeling that they were no longer there – not the men I had been chatting to and laughing with. Their outer shells, so to speak, were all that was left of them. At the same time I had a feeling of utter abhorrence of war, of its stupidity and waste. I just felt hopping mad at the whole crazy business. Geoffrey Studdert Kennedy expressed his feelings and mine, too, in the piece of verse called 'Waste' in the collection of his poetry, 'The Unutterable Beauty':

Waste
'Waste of Muscle, waste of Brain,
Waste of Patience, waste of Pain,
Waste of Manhood, waste of Health,
Waste of Beauty, waste of Wealth,
Waste of Blood, and waste of Tears,
Waste of Youth's most precious years,
Waste of ways the Saints have trod,
Waste of Glory, waste of God, – War!'

Joining in the job of digging graves for these men, not an easy job in such stony ground and in the growing heat of a September morning, helped to get rid of a bit of anger, and take one's mind off the senselessness of it all but my horror was suddenly brought back as we attempted to carry and drag one of the men into the shallow grave we had managed to dig. A marine took his head and shoulders and I took his legs. It was like picking up a suit of clothes by the shoulders and the legs. It was heavy but it just gave in the middle, his back was shot away.

There had been a tremendous amount of activity that previous night but it wasn't until later that we learned that the Royal Navy had poured in some heavy shells from one of the battle ships. Our men were no distance from the German position, as I learned for myself when I attempted to cross a road to a white-washed cottage. Fortunately our marines saw what I was about to do and called out "watch out Padre that road's mined". Whether the Germans heard them shouting or whether they had spotted some movement, or had heard our digging I don't know, but it was at that juncture that a lot of tracer came in our direction and set fire to a thicket on our right. I felt that was probably my cue to leave the locality.

I was making my way down that hill and was approaching our lines as the dark was falling and happened to walk in front of a well camouflaged 25-pounder just as it fired. I quite literally reeled, both from sheer fright and from the ear-splitting crack. I believe this is why for many years I've been unable to get the gist of a conversation very clearly and am unable to pick up high-pitched notes, which may be a blessing in disguise where telephone and door bells are concerned, but I'm sorry to miss the bird song. At length in my old age I have acquired a hearing aid!

So very much happened in those September days. It might have been the same day that I buried two more of our unit, a marine and our Second-in-Command. The latter had been Adjutant, but when our Second-in-Command had been killed on the beach in our landings in Sicily, the Adjutant took his place as Second-in-Command. I mention his death because I had never before seen a completely bloodless corpse. He had lain out most of the night and must have lost every drop of blood in his body: he was the colour of cream! I had married him to a Wren Officer only a few weeks before we sailed from the Clyde in June.

CHAPTER NINE

Through the Valley

At Troon, before we sailed, I had asked a chippy chap in the unit if he would knock me up a simple wooden cross. I wanted one that could be dismantled into a base, an upright and a horizontal so that it could be packed without difficulty. He very quickly made an excellent cross. Unfortunately when we landed in Sicily we lost all our gear except that in which we went ashore. So I had to ask my carpenter friend if he could knock me up a similar cross to the one he had made for me in Scotland. It wasn't many days before he had produced another cross, which was used every time we were able to hold a service.

There's a somewhat sad end to the story of the cross. On one of those days towards the end of September when the incessant crump of mortar fire reverberated between the hills and the German and Allied machine guns seemed to be stuttering non-stop, a marine asked me to go to his mate who was dying, if not already dead. We found him, with both feet blown off and only the stumps left. I think he must have been answering a call of nature at the time because his trousers were down. I was sorry to find that it was my friend the carpenter who had been acting as a runner – a messenger. We buried him beside a walnut tree. Then it came to my turn to knock up a simple cross to put up over his grave, just two stout sticks tied together stuck in the ground, with his helmet hung on top.

Twenty five years later on Salerno day at Bickleigh HQ of 41 Commando Royal Marines, I was asked to preach at the Parade Service. I related this story of the carpenter who had twice made a cross for me, and went on to tell of my making a cross for him. I then linked it all up with the Carpenter of Nazareth who gave himself in the service of others.

After the service a man came up to me and said "I helped you to dig that grave; he was my mate".

Once, during a fairly concentrated attack of mortar fire on a road up a hillside, I was tempted to take shelter with 3 or 4 marines who were safely tucked under a truck. It was when I realised it was an ammunition truck that I decided to carry on walking. I still have a vivid memory of watching and waiting for the crump of each mortar bomb and trying to work out where the next one would land as I carried on up the hill.

Late one afternoon I was making my way back to our sick bay from a hill to the North East of Salerno where I had been burying a number of our dead. The road wound its way down the hillside and I could just discern in the distance a narrowing of the track where the valley seemed to become steeper and where it took a sharp bend. The Germans were directing their fire fairly accurately onto this point as a burning truck or two showed. I was tempted to stay where I was, but the shadows were already lengthening and there was still some distance to go and I didn't like the idea of staying up on the hillside for the night without a meal or a blanket. I decided to risk it and walk on through the valley but I was very frightened.

On many occasions since then when using the 23rd Psalm at worship or at weddings or funerals, the words "Though I walk through the valley of the shadow of death" have momentarily taken me back to that particular experience at Salerno.

One morning a Corporal in the transport section asked me to go up with him to try to find and bury one of our men he thought had been killed. There had been a good deal of enemy activity and as well as mortar bombs, shells were dropping and I recall hearing the whine of a shell and trying to bury myself as half an oak tree came crashing down just in front of us. I took a run and a jump into the nearest slit trench I could see. I realised too late that it was already occupied by a couple of chaps on one of whom I landed somewhat heavily.

As I did so I thought I spotted a strip of red on his uniform: it was Sir Robert Laycock, then Brigadier Bob Laycock, CO of the Special Service Brigade, later to become Chief of Combined Operations and then Governor of Malta. He was very decent about it and gave me a warm welcome with "what the bloody hell are you doing here Padre?" Later I received the following letter from him:

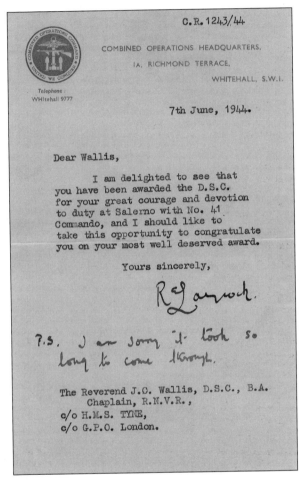

C.R. 1243/44

COMBINED OPERATIONS HEADQUARTERS,
1A, RICHMOND TERRACE,
WHITEHALL, S.W.1.

Telephone :
WHitehall 9777

7th June, 1944.

Dear Wallis,

I am delighted to see that you have been awarded the D.S.C. for your great courage and devotion to duty at Salerno with No. 41 Commando, and I should like to take this opportunity to congratulate you on your most well deserved award.

Yours sincerely,

R Laycock.

P.S. I am sorry I took so long to come through.

The Reverend J.C. Wallis, D.S.C., B.A.
Chaplain, R.N.V.R.,
c/o H.M.S. TYNE,
c/o G.P.O. London.

It was after this meeting with Bob Laycock that we found the man who was thought to have been wounded, if not dead. He must have received the blast of an exploding mortar bomb which knocked him out completely. He had been laid in the bottom of a slit trench and given the treatment for shock: warmth in the shape of a heavy blanket and covered with his mackintosh cape. In the heat of September in Southern Italy the consequence was that when we uncovered him he was steaming, and it was as if he had just got out of a hot bath. He seemed to be none the worse and this man, a Corporal then, continued in the Corps after the war reaching the rank of Colonel. He was a very brave man and served with distinction in some of the trouble spots of the post-war world.

CHAPTER TEN

Last Days in Salerno

It was on a Friday afternoon towards the end of September that a group of us were gathered in a cave in a hillside, as depressed and as hopeless a lot as you can imagine. We were so afraid that the unit would be required to put in yet another attack that night and we knew we were utterly incapable of doing it. We had lost so many officers and men: most of our Troop Commanders had been killed or wounded or were missing and we seemed to be down to a few Second Lieutenants. The Sergeant with us that afternoon was quite obviously shell-shocked and the MO and myself were both non-combatants. As I looked out of the entrance of the cave I saw a figure walking across the fields in our direction. He was a Captain in the Ox & Bucks and had come to tell us that his unit – I think it was the 5th Battalion – would be relieving us. To say we all felt profoundly thankful would have been the understatement of the year.

We went back down the hills to the coast with the same sort of feeling one had when beginning one's leave. I was certainly looking forward to a bit of rest and relaxation and I think we all were. I got my rest and refreshment in hospital; Malaria reared its ugly head again!

On the Sunday morning following our relief the intelligence officer and I had decided we'd have a bathe. We were halfway down a fairly shallow cliff path when an Italian woman started shouting at us from above "Mina, mina", but it wasn't until we saw a large red notice ahead of us with MINA on it that we realised what she was on about. Having managed most of the descent without being blown up we felt we might risk the remainder. Had we strayed off the path things might have been different. It was a great joy to throw off shirt and shorts and plunge into the sea.

All went swimmingly until we saw two large and very low-flying aircraft coming along the water's edge towards us.

We soon knew they weren't ours because there was that horrible rat-at-at-at-at and the more horrible line of splashes on the sea's surface, obviously intended for us. We instinctively ducked under the water but by then they had passed us.

It wasn't long before they were back again repeating the procedure and we too again made ourselves invisible. After 2 or 3 runs they gave up and we came out. Although the water was not cold I suppose it was the length of time we had to spend in it that brought out the Malaria again.

I was taken first to a Field Dressing Station and then to a tented hospital which was full of battle casualties from the heavy fighting. The mosquitoes were very much in evidence but fortunately the mosquito nets saved us from their round-the-clock dive bombing.

It was while I was there that I was relieved of several bits of 'loot' which I had acquired, my prize possession was an Italian water bottle which held more than the British type and the insulation kept the water just a fraction cooler than our bottles. A very nice Italian black shirt also disappeared and several other bits and pieces.

I was flown by an old and very uncomfortable Douglas Dakota to a hospital in Catania in Sicily. I well remember my first night there: leaning over the wash basin and being very, very sick from the large doses of Mepacrine, the only sort of quinine available. As I had been wearing khaki shirt and shorts when I was admitted, the sister on the small ward of 4 beds, occupied by 3 Army officers and myself, insisted that an Italian barber should come and shave off the beard I had grown over the past few months.

I had a lot of trouble convincing him that he wasn't going to shave off the beard. I had almost as much trouble convincing the sister that I was a Naval Chaplain.

The four of us in this small ward used to pull our beds together as best we could and we played bridge interminably.

When I was considered to be free from malaria I was taken to an officers Red Cross convalescent establishment in the Hotel San Pancrazio at Taormina. It was a beautiful place for a week or two's holiday. An old Sicilian village at the top of the cliffs with a view of Mount Etna on one side and the Mediterranean on the other. It was a fairly steep walk down to the beach but the bathing was good and one could hire a boat and row out to coral caves. There was also a beach hut where we used to play bridge. We had time to walk and to visit further afield in transport put at our disposal, up the coast to Messina and inland to some of the hill villages.

At the end of the unit's short period in action, according to my records, fifty-four officers and men were killed, one hundred and thirty-nine wounded and eleven taken prisoner-of-war. I quote a passage from 'A Student in Arms', a book published in 1916, describing the men of a Kitchener battalion and their attitude to action in Flanders. I'm sure a great deal of this is true, not only of the men who gave their lives in the Great War of 1914-18, but of those who served in the 1939-45 War. This passage may strike many today as sentimental, emotional, exaggerated – as mere heroics – but there is underlying it something that expresses what I can't put into words which I feel towards those men of 41 Royal Marine Commando, with whom I served in Sicily and at Salerno, men with whom I lived for a year or two and whose company I enjoyed and whom I looked on as friends, a number of whom were wounded and to quite a few of whom I gave Christian burial.

"Their spirits effervesced. Their wit sparkled. Hunger and thirst could not depress them. Rain could not damp them. Cold could not chill them. Every hardship became a joke. They did not endure hardship, they derided it. Never was such a triumph of spirit over matter. As for death, it was, in a way, the greatest joke of all. In a way, for if it was another fellow that was hit, it was an occasion for tenderness and grief. But if one of them was hit: O Death, where is thy sting? O Grave where is thy victory? Portentous, solemn death, you looked a fool when you tackled one of them! Life? They did not value life. They had never been able to make much of a fist of it. But if they lived amiss, they died gloriously. With a smile for the pain and the dread of it. With a gay heart they gave their greatest gift and with a smile to think that after all they had anything to give which was of value."

CHAPTER ELEVEN

Africa

Meanwhile my unit had been transferred to North Africa, to Tunisia, first to Bizerta and then to a transit camp at Bone. I managed to link up with them and found them somewhat low in morale. Christmas was approaching and there seemed little hope of returning to England and there was nothing much to do in Tunisia. We began making preparations for Christmas and then came the morning when the MO happened to be standing next to me in the heads – the loo. He took one look at me, or rather at what I was doing and said "Padre, you've got jaundice".

I was again whisked off to hospital, and this time it was a Canadian hospital. By the evening my head was splitting, my throat was terribly sore and again I was very, very sick. I spent about 14 days in that hospital and once I had got over the nausea I quite enjoyed my stay.

There was a fine library of paperbacks and I was getting through a novel a day. At night we were often kept awake by the noise of the rats running in the roof space of the large Nissen hut which was our ward. In the bed next to mine was an army doctor. One evening when we had managed to get hold of a bottle of Guinness, he suggested we keep a little back until the morning and when we had to offer up our specimens we added our little drop of Guinness which made the hospital MO a bit dubious about our recovery.

In our ditch at Salerno I had got to know a couple of New Zealanders who were now stationed somewhere near us in Tunisia and they came to visit me. Upon seeing that all my belongings were stuffed into a kit bag I kept under the bed, they very kindly made me a large wooden suitcase which proved extremely useful until we arrived back in England. They also brought me a pipe bowl of Algerian briar root which they had turned on a lathe and to which I fixed a stem when I got home. It was one of the finest pipes I ever smoked.

I was discharged a few days before Christmas and returned to my unit in the transit camp at Bone and began making preparations for Christmas. There wasn't much we could do, perhaps some sort of Christmas concert, a Carol Service and a good Christmas dinner. Life seemed so purposeless in that camp; we had no idea how long we were to remain there and we wondered if anyone was aware that we were there, and although the food and the conditions were fairly good, morale was poor.

The climate didn't help; at midday the sun was really hot and we were happy to strip to the waist. At night it became very cold and one had to scrounge extra blankets. It sometimes rained and the drainage wasn't too efficient so that if one had to leave the tent in the darkness for a call of nature it meant immediately getting one's feet wet in the mini-moat that had been dug round the tent to lead the rain water away.

Some of my fellow officers used to get away from camp to dine at a hotel just outside Bone. I went with them once but wasn't impressed enough to repeat the visit. I was always tucked up in my camp bed and had probably been asleep for an hour or more when they returned. There was one in particular who pretended he was always most concerned for my well-being. "Now Padre, are you sure you're warm enough? Would you like me to get you another blanket?" The first night this happened I was quite impressed but when it became a regular feature of the party's return I realised it was probably due more to the brandy than to this man's care for his padre.

One morning the buzz went round the camp that we were returning home. Of course we thought it was someone's idea of a joke, but it wasn't and we were ordered to be ready at fairly short notice to embark on a convoy of troop carrying trucks to take us to Algiers. We were issued with our rations: bully-beef and biscuits and bread. I sat up next to the driver in one of the trucks. The scenery was wonderful and in places awesome with the deep ravines and the mountainous nature of a good deal of the route.

One or two memories stand out: the sudden darkness that came upon us as we were travelling through the wide open spaces of the fields. It lasted only for a few seconds and

61

then the light and sun was restored. It was caused by colossal flocks of birds, starlings I suppose they were, as in their thousands they swooped overhead. Standing round the bonfire we made with wood from the huts we broke up on the hillside at Setif on Christmas Eve. Singing carols and trying to keep warm and marvelling at the brightness of the stars in the frosty atmosphere. I think most of the men will remember Christmas Eve on that hillside at Setif.

We eventually arrived at Algiers on Christmas Day in the afternoon. I have a vivid memory of hundreds of oranges running wild in the street from a barrow overturned by some of our fellows who had for some reason taken a dislike to its owner.

We were put into the stadium at Algiers, to await orders to board SS *Otranto*. Although we had been given bully-beef and biscuits and some bread when we set out from Bone, it didn't last as long as we would have wished. Joe Barrett, our QM and a real friend of mine gave me the sign to follow him and when we had found a bit of privacy in a corridor away from the mob, Joe produced a tin of bully-beef and a tin of peaches and we had an unexpectedly fine Christmas dinner. This was typical of Joe's ingenuity.

At length we were taken to the Docks to board our ship for home. A unit was still disembarking at one end as we embarked at the other. It was very much overcrowded as far as sleeping accommodation was concerned and we were in bunks of three tiers with not very much room between them. There was a good deal of noise at night, not merely snoring but from men who were suffering nightmares from their recent experiences.

Nevertheless it was a heavenly trip with good food and drink. Some of us felt it a pity that we had to go all the way to Greenock to be off-loaded, and then to have the long uncomfortable journey to the south, not even to our homes, but to the Royal Marines Depot at Deal. It seemed strange to see snow and ice all around.

From Deal we were given leave and dozens of letters which we had been deprived of for some weeks. Towards the end of my leave I received a telegram from the Adjutant telling me to report back to Deal. I was really furious when I discovered it was because three bridge players who were still in barracks couldn't find a 4th so they sent for the parson.

I had made arrangements with the Admiralty for the use of a car with a Wren driver to visit some of the next-of-kin of our many casualties. I tried to group them as far as possible round the centres of London, Liverpool and Manchester. It was a harrowing experience but it was one of the more worthwhile things I did during the war. I couldn't help feeling that parents, especially mothers, were more deeply affected than widows, although the young East End widow of one of our sergeants, married only a few months, was still obviously suffering numbness from her sudden and unexpected widowhood.

As I was going out of the room of an elderly couple I visited at Guildford, the father pointed to a pair of shoes in the corner, soled and heeled and a lump came to my throat as he said "I had them done for when he came on leave, but he won't need them now".

After our leave we were transferred to Ramsgate, finding our own accommodation as we did earlier in our history. It was while we were there that I attended a conference of Navy, Army and Airforce Chaplains at Canterbury and had the privilege of meeting and listening to the Archbishop, William Temple.

I usually managed to spend a night or two in London during a leave to go to a theatre and to meet up with a few friends. Shortly after our return from the Med I was walking along Kings Road, Chelsea and was aware that some people were tending to look twice at me. I didn't realise at the time but I suppose my uniform did present a bit of a problem and I might well have been taken for a 5th Columnist. I was in Khaki Service Dress but was wearing a beard, something not allowed in the Army except, so I've been told, for a Sgt Major in one of the Scottish Regiments. I was wearing the Green Beret, with a Naval Officer's badge and a Royal Navy shoulder flash under a Maltese Cross, the only sign of rank, or lack of it, of a Naval chaplain. No wonder people looked twice.

I had arranged to go into Retreat for a few days at the Cowley Fathers House, The Society of St John the Evangelist at Westminster and while there I received a posting from the Admiralty to HMS *Tyne*. I had no idea what she was or where she was, but I was assured by my senior chaplain, Royal Marines, that I was very fortunate to get such a good posting.

CHAPTER TWELVE

Home Waters

It was in early March 1944 that I set off for Scapa Flow, a journey which took about 36 hours. The trains were over-crowded and cold and we saw scarcely anything of the countryside because the windows were covered with snow and dirt. It was an uncomfortable trip and it was a relief when at last we reached Thurso. The crossing of the Pentland Firth made the train journey seem like a luxury trip. I had no idea what a shocking stretch of water it is: the wind was blowing the snow horizontally and the crossing to Kirkwall was a rough one to say the least, most of the passengers went inside or below to get out of the freezing cold but with a naval coat buttoned up to the neck the wind and the snow didn't seem to matter. My aim was to avoid seasickness, which I was able to do in spite of all the symptoms. It was a relief to get aboard HMS Tyne, a destroyer depot ship, a floating workshop. I found it almost too good to be true to be shown to my own cabin, with hot and cold water laid on, an electric radiator, a desk and a bunk with white sheets! This was indeed luxurious compared to one's life as a RM Commando. It gave me a good opportunity to use this contrast in Sermons when there was a certain amount of discontent among the large ship's company at what they felt was their dismal lot at Scapa away from civilisation.

One soon settled into life aboard. There was a fine ship's chapel aft, but unfortunately men had to come through the officers' quarters to get to it and they had to be fairly keen if they wanted to come to Holy Communion either on Sunday or on weekdays. I was immensely impressed on my first few Sundays to see such a large turn out of the more senior officers at Holy Communion: the Admiral, his Flag Lieutenant and Secretary and most of his staff: the Captain of the ship, the Paymaster Captain, the PMO. Our daily celebrations of HC were usually attended by a Server and per-

haps one or two others. We used to have an evening service on Sundays which I felt was well worthwhile: it seemed to speak of home and of one's family and loved ones. After the early Sunday Holy Communion in HMS Tyne, a quick breakfast and then morning service in the Recreation space. The ship produced a good band and the singing was good too. The Navy had three hymn cards with all the old favourites, but we sang some canticles as well because we used a shortened form of Matins. One Sunday we had just sung the first part of the verse of the Venite which begins "The sea is His" and I heard from someone in the rear of the congregation "and he can keep it".

HMS Tyne, 'in her warpaint'. A Destroyer Depot Ship, she served in the Home fleet from 1941-1944 and the British Pacific Fleet during the last year of the war.

After Morning Service in HMS *Tyne* I would set off for services in the destroyers, sometimes Holy Communion but more often a morning service followed by Holy Communion. These were always arranged with the destroyer's Captain during one's visiting in the previous week. It made a somewhat heavy Sunday forenoon; often two or three services, one after another, as well as the two services in *Tyne*. It was good to get back for lunch and a rest. Each day, either on the Fo'c's'le or the Quarter deck we had prayers with a hymn usually accompanied by a Fiddler standing up on the Capstan. When anything like a sea was running it was fascinating to watch the rows of sailors, lined up on each side of the ship, facing inboard, moving with the motion of the

66

ship. A lurch to starboard and all would take a step backwards or forwards according to which side they were on, but carrying on singing as if nothing was happening. An incident that occurred at a Sunday morning service in *Tyne* is worth recording.

I treasured a sermon I heard as a boy, preached by a Missions to Seamen Chaplain about the King's drinking horn which had inscribed round it words from 117th verse of the 119th Psalm "Hold thou me up and I shall be safe". I had just announced this as my text when there was a tremendous commotion in a certain section of the congregation and we discovered that a bench on which five sailors were sitting had collapsed and they found themselves sprawling in a heap on the deck. I suggested that this catastrophe supported the owner of the drinking horn and the writer of the Psalm and that the assembled Company might learn something from this apparent coincidence.

In the middle of June I had received the following letter from the Admiralty:

Notification of the award of the Distinguished Service Cross. Chaplain of the Fleet.

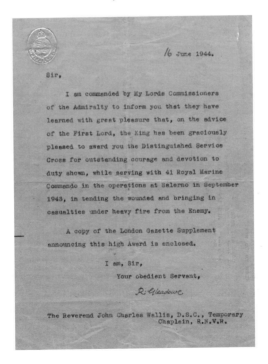

/6 June 1944.

Sir,

I am commended by My Lords Commissioners of the Admiralty to inform you that they have learned with great pleasure that, on the advice of the First Lord, the King has been graciously pleased to award you the Distinguished Service Cross for outstanding courage and devotion to duty shown, while serving with 41 Royal Marine Commando in the operations at Salerno in September 1943, in tending the wounded and bringing in casualties under heavy fire from the Enemy.

A copy of the London Gazette Supplement announcing this high Award is enclosed.

I am, Sir,

Your obedient Servant,

R. Gleadowe.

The Reverend John Charles Wallis, D.S.C., Temporary Chaplain, R.N.V.R.

And one from the Chaplain of the Fleet:

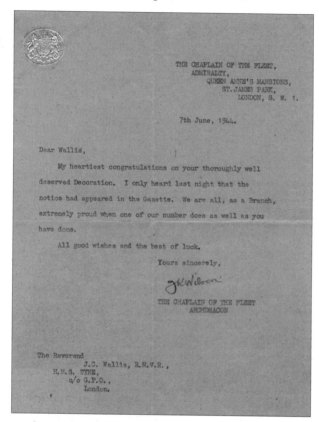

THE CHAPLAIN OF THE FLEET,
ADMIRALTY,
QUEEN ANNE'S MANSIONS,
ST. JAMES PARK,
LONDON, S. W. 1.

7th June, 1944.

Dear Wallis,

My heartiest congratulations on your thoroughly well deserved Decoration. I only heard last night that the notice had appeared in the Gazette. We are all, as a Branch, extremely proud when one of our number does as well as you have done.

All good wishes and the best of luck.

Yours sincerely,

J.K. Wilson

THE CHAPLAIN OF THE FLEET
ARCHDEACON

The Reverend
J.C. Wallis, R.N.V.R.,
H.M.S. TYNE,
c/o G.P.O.,
London.

Below: *John* (fifth from the left) *presented, with other award winners, to His Majesty King George VI on the deck of* HMS Tyne *during the spring of 1944.*

His Majesty King George VI visited us at Scapa and I felt privileged to be presented to him on the Quarter deck with about ten other officers who had received awards but owing, as they say, to the exigencies of the service would be unable to attend the next investiture at Buckingham Palace as we would not still be in home waters. Instead it was sent to me by post with the following letter from His Majesty:

BUCKINGHAM PALACE

I greatly regret that I am unable to give you personally the award which you have so well earned.

I now send it to you with my congratulations and my best wishes for your future happiness.

(signed) George RI

Right: *one from the King too!*

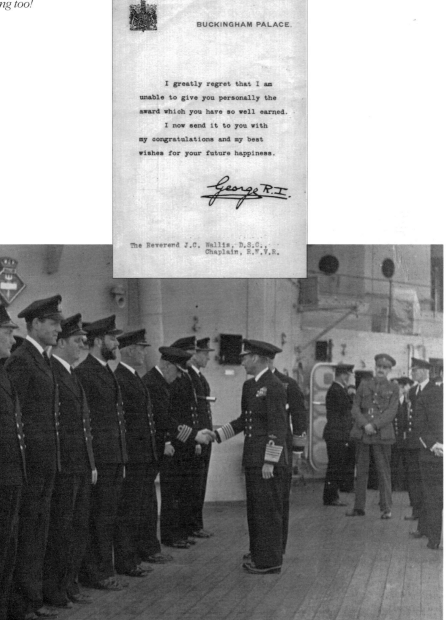

BUCKINGHAM PALACE.

I greatly regret that I am
unable to give you personally the
award which you have so well earned.
I now send it to you with
my congratulations and my best
wishes for your future happiness.

George R.I.

The Reverend J.C. Wallis, D.S.C.,
Chaplain, R.N.V.R.

Another memorable visit was from General Montgomery who attended Sunday morning service in HMS *Tyne*. When I prepared my talk I had no idea that he would be present otherwise I might have thought twice on the subject of the great men of history: the would-be World's military conquerors. Caesar, Alexander the Great, Napoleon, Adolph Hitler and how they stood in comparison with Jesus of Nazareth. In the Wardroom after the service many chaps seemed to be of the opinion that I was intending to take the mickey out of Monty. He gave no impression of suspicion on this score and appeared quite eager to continue with the subject.

I gathered that Scapa Flow was much the same as it had been during the Great War. Our 'postie' (postman) in *Tyne* had served his time in the Royal Navy and had known Scapa as it then was. He came from the parish in Wiltshire where I had served as curate and was a member of our branch of Toc H in Trowbridge. We formed a branch of Toc H in Tyne and held weekly meetings at which we were fortunate in being able to draw on some first class speakers from among the large number of officers we carried, all specialists in their subjects. Another regular weekly meeting was of the Classical Music Society which met in the ship's Chapel to listen to a selection of the hundreds of records which had been built up. It was a popular occasion and usually every inch of floor space was used as seating accommodation and it gave many of us a love of the Classics and helped many through those somewhat dreary days. We usually had two or three destroyers alongside us, 'our babies', as we called them, undergoing repairs, so there were always opportunities for the Chaplain to do a bit of visiting.

We were able to get eggs from the small holdings in the Orkneys and it wasn't long before I had packed a large biscuit tin with saw-dust and far too many eggs and sent it off to my parents. My father said he received two unbroken eggs plus an appalling mess.

After a few months at Scapa we sailed south to join the colossal amount of shipping which had built up in the Solent for the coming invasion of Normandy. Action stations sounded as we were ploughing through the Irish Sea. I use the word ploughing because it was at the height of the June

Above: *Fleet destroyers in line ahead. 'Our babies' as they were know by the crew of the Destroyer Depot Ship.*

gales and once or twice I thought the ship must break her back. I had taken up my action station right aft, a couple of decks down and was very conscious of the whipping of the tail end. The all clear was sounded and when we went up on deck we were staggered at the hundreds of ships and craft of all descriptions lying between the Coast of Dorset and Hampshire and the Isle of Wight as far as the eye could see. One felt it would be possible to walk across to the Island on the ships.

We were all a bit apprehensive. We felt sure the Germans wouldn't miss an opportunity like this and we thought we would be bombed and dive-bombed at any moment. I went ashore one day at Portsmouth and took a bus to Southampton to see my sister. All through the countryside were thousands of vehicles, tanks and guns and dozens of ammunition dumps.

I had made a date with the skipper of one of our destroyers and he was going to take me the next day over to Arramanche but for some reason either he or I had to call off. I

71

was fortunate because that destroyer hit a mine and broke in two.

Soon after we anchored between Ryde and Portsmouth I managed to get a trip in a destroyer that was taking Admiral Ramsay from Portsmouth to Arromanche. The channel was still quite tempestuous and one felt sorry for all personnel who had been taken over to Normandy in flat bottomed landing craft. I worked on the assumption that the more air one can get the less one feels the motion, so I climbed up to the signal deck. Looking ahead it seemed to me that the ship was going through the waves rather than over them. Having felt decidedly queer for some time I came to the conclusion that I simply couldn't last any longer and that at any moment I was going to be very sick. I didn't fancy doing this in the presence of the buntings – the signal men – so I found a bucket and having been assured that no one else needed it at the moment and that I could help myself, I took it out of sight, sat down on something or other with the bucket between my knees and I could have been as sick as I liked in complete privacy. From that moment I didn't want to be sick and what is more descended 3 or 4 decks to the small stuffy wardroom and beginning with a plateful of fairly greasy soup had a decent lunch. I've never quite understood that incident. There must be some psychology in it somewhere. Nor have I understood why I have never been sea-sick. Even when making our landing in Sicily in those flat bottomed landing craft when I think everyone of the other 34 men in my craft were being sick and the stench was simply horrible, I wasn't sick. Again later in the Pacific with those long smooth rollers when I felt distinctly ill I was never sick. I might have felt better had I been.

One morning quite early Captain D of one of the destroyer flotillas came somewhat breathlessly into my cabin to ask me to come aboard his ship which had just returned from the Normandy coast to lead a short service of thanksgiving for their deliverance from a torpedo attack. Apparently a torpedo had been spotted coming for the ship; the Captain had immediately been informed and with tremendous presence of mind had ordered the ship to be turned so that the bows faced the on-coming torpedo which meant that it glanced alongside the destroyer, but its warhead didn't strike any part. The Captain wanted the ship's company to thank God for their deliverance.

It was while we were lying off Spithead that I was awakened by a most strange noise, which I couldn't place at all. It wasn't a ship and it wasn't an aircraft: it sounded more like an express train passing overhead. I jumped out of my bunk and into my slippers and dressing gown and ran up on deck, where there were a number of officers equally puzzled. We soon spotted the source of the noise: small flaming objects which we came to know as V Ones. We soon learned that immediately the noise stopped the object fell. This was the first we had seen or heard of Hitler's new weapon. The fleet wasn't hit; most of those we saw that night fell behind Portsmouth.

We eventually returned to Scapa Flow in August 1944 but it wasn't long before we sailed down to the Clyde, not so much for a refit, but as we realised later, for sundry alterations to make the ship more amenable to weather warmer than it had been used to at Scapa. Most of the ship's company was given leave and I recall the horrible feeling of emptiness in the ship when one returned from an evening ashore in Glasgow.

I enjoyed a very pleasant leave in Wiltshire in August and spent another week in London in October. I was travelling north to rejoin my ship and by 10pm had reached Perth. Feeling in need of food I was walking along the platform in search of it when I was shaken by a voice over the SRE. "Will Padre Wallis report to the RTO forthwith". I was told that I had eleven days embarkation leave and was to rejoin the ship at Greenock at the end of that leave. Why I wasn't told this before I left Euston no-one seemed to know. There was no train back to London before morning so I had to find supper, bed and breakfast in an hotel and catch the early morning train south.

CHAPTER THIRTEEN

We Sail East

We sailed early in November from the Clyde and we realised we were going East. It made a change to go through the Bay of Biscay and the Mediterranean without fear of enemy opposition and to see something of the Moroccan coast and the Atlas Mountains, Algiers and Bone where I had been a year before. We passed Cyrenaica and Libya and Alexandria and came to Port Said where we were given shore leave. We did a bit of shopping at Simon Artz and had supper at an hotel, entertained by a Gilli-Gilli man and his Chicks.

I was surprised how narrow the Suez Canal appeared to be but HMS *Tyne*, not a small ship, managed to get through quite comfortably and we anchored for some hours in Suez Bay, sizzling in the heat. From what I saw of the Sinai peninsula made me feel sympathetic towards the Israelites; 40 years in that sort of barren mountainous terrain and sweltering climate would test anyone. If we thought the Gulf of Suez was hot we found the Red Sea even hotter. The fact that we were ordered into Tropical Rig made little difference. We found Aden a relief with a trip to Old Aden which stank somewhat and a visit to the Queen of Sheba's water tanks. We played a game of hockey at Aden which only served to increase what we had already found to be an insatiable thirst. We spent a week in the Indian Ocean and eventually arrived at Ceylon and entered Colombo Harbour. What struck me almost immediately as I went ashore in a launch was the tremendous wing-span of the huge butterflies which skimmed over the water all around us. A couple of days sailing from Colombo brought us to Trincomalee, a beautiful spot.

Trincomalee was a Dutch possession at one time as was a good deal of territory around the Indian Ocean. Fort Frederick was a delightful spot on the coast, with a swimming pool protected from the huge rollers which would otherwise have made life difficult for bathers. The parkland surrounding the Fort was full of deer. It had a fine church where we held a Christmas Carol Service, a combined Services effort of Navy, Army and Air Force. The Captain's secretary, Scratch, as he was called, was married there to a Wren who flew in from Mombassa and the reception was held aboard our ship. It was in Trinco that I bought a box of cheroots which I didn't open until I arrived home. I found I couldn't get on with them; they were green, but for some reason I kept the box in a drawer in my desk. It must have been 20 years later that my two young daughters found them and apparently enjoyed them.

One afternoon I was bathing on the main beach with hundreds of Army and Navy personnel. The breakers were coming in fairly high and I thought it would be fun to get out beyond them before they broke and to surf ride in to the beach on one of them. I soon found myself on the seaward side of them but instead of riding one home I found myself being dragged further and further out. The more I put into the effort of trying to get back to the beach the more I puffed and blowed and the further away the line of breaking waves seemed to get. I was very near to panic and then I saw a head in the water and swam up to it hoping its owner might have given me a helping hand. Instead he clutched at me and said: "For God's sake help me mate". All I could suggest was that we swam parallel with the beach aiming for a headland that jutted out from the beach a mile or so away, hoping we might be washed up on it. After swimming slowly along for some time I was suddenly aware that I was being lifted high on the crest of a breaker and I thought "thank goodness, this means we are getting towards the beach", but in that very second I was flung down and hit the sea bed with some force. I thought I was never going to surface but came up just in time to see another towering wave curling down on top of me, a really horrible and frightening sight. Fortunately this one pushed me horizontally towards the beach rather than downwards and I realised I was safe at last. What happened to the other chap I don't know, it really was a matter of each man for himself. The horror of that breaker curling over and enveloping me formed the basis of nightmares for some years.

After two months in Trincomalee we sailed for Australia. Father Neptune came aboard for the day when we crossed the line and we all received the traditional ducking. We spent a day in Freemantle and I was impressed to see that one of the first people up the gangway was the Missions to Seamen Chaplain. A truck or two on the quayside brought us all gifts from the Mission: soap, razor blades, socks, scarves, grapes etc. I took the opportunity to visit Perth, chiefly to buy some song sheets from Boozey and Hawkes for the Madrigal Group we had collected on board. Perth was a beautiful city and I've often described it as being like an English Cathedral City. We sailed across the Great Australian Bight to Sydney and were thrilled to tie up alongside Circular Quay, which meant we were able to step ashore into the centre of Sydney. The local branch of Toc H very quickly made contact with me and on the first evening I was taken out to dinner and then to a Symphony Concert in the Town Hall. Within a week they had made arrangements for some of us to spend a few days at Katoomba in the Blue Mountains.

After this week of rehabilitation, or fun and games, we sailed up the East Coast of Australia to Manus in the Admiralty Islands, $1^1/_2$ degrees off the Equator and horribly humid. We spent only a couple of weeks there before sailing for Leyte in the Philippines where one or two trips ashore were enough to satisfy one's curiosity. Although it was extremely hot, at least it was a dry heat, but after two months we were glad to put to sea again and after a short call at Manus we were on our way again for "the land of our dreams" Sydney, where a warm welcome awaited us and where we were feted with visits here and there and meals everywhere. Toc H looked after me well, as did a Sydney stockbroker whom I had somehow got to know, and a man who ran a Sydney newspaper. I spent a night or two at Bowral where Sir Donald Bradman used to play cricket and took the opportunity of visiting Canberra. One Sunday I was invited to preach in Sydney Cathedral and to dine with the Archbishop and his wife. On the day before we sailed north again to what we knew would be a very much less pleasant existence than the last month had been, the Archbishop came on board to preach. He was a large, tall figure and he stood before those

Sidney Harbour 1945. HMS Tyne may just be observed off the point of land.

hundreds of sailors and announced his text "When thou passest through the waters I will be with thee". I think we were all impressed by his message.

After a night or two in Manus we sailed for the Marshall Islands to join the 38th Task Force of the American Fleet at Eniwetock. We used to go ashore to swim and to get some iced beer from the American NAAFI. One had to be sure to get the mouth over the hole in the can when it was opened, otherwise it would shoot up to the top of the palm trees! In order to collect the beer an officer had to be with the party to sign for the cans according to the numbers of sailors in the party. On one occasion, against my better judgment I was persuaded by my thirsty lot, 12 in number, to ask for 36 cans. I felt humiliated and conscience-stricken when the Yank in charge said he felt it strange that a Royal Naval Chaplain couldn't count. We used to get a tremendous number of tropical rainstorms which we welcomed because they helped to cool us down. We would often strip off and walk the Quarter Deck. If we were ashore the sand would be inundated in no time but within a few minutes it was all

77

Two Old Tauntonians. John with Sir John Butters who was Chief Commissioner of Canberra 1924-1929.

soaked up and the sand as dry as dust again. The steam had to be seen to be believed. A tropical storm at night was accompanied by the most wonderful display of forked lightning with the tremendous cracks that always went with it.

Some of us were invited to a meal aboard an American hospital ship. We were impressed more with the air conditioning than with the food, although that was good and a pleasant change from our usual fare, but to sit for an hour or two in comfort and to know again what it was like not to have a wet shirt clinging to one's back: it was sheer joy!

Two prevalent and painful complaints were Dhobi's itch and Athlete's foot.

After a month in the Marshall Islands we spent another month at Manus and it was while we were there on this visit in August 1945 that we heard of the dropping of the Atom

78

bomb on Hiroshima. I managed to get several interesting trips ashore to various small islands. One, I think it was in those days called Pitylou, had been a Copra estate or plantation, but it had been neglected during the war years. I was shaken considerably to see the whole beach on which we had landed moving. It was covered with hermit crabs, hundreds, thousands of them and they were all on the move. I had another experience of hermit crabs. I had been watching some squids on one of the beaches on Manus and I realised that there were some really beautiful sea-shells around. Unfortunately I had nothing to carry them in and all I had on was bathing trunks, so I started putting the shells in my bathing shorts. It wasn't long before I was being nipped quite painfully in a very sensitive part of me and on taking my trunks down I discovered a baby hermit crab was in occupation of one of the small shells.

Some of us went ashore one afternoon in the Engineers cutter; the object was to see how far we could get up the river which flowed into the sea almost opposite where our ship was anchored. We could see the sand-bar and the entrance through binoculars. The sand-bar proved to be a real bar and even the shallow cutter couldn't find a passage through. We concluded that the only course was to leave one man in the boat and the rest of us to swim for it. This raised the nasty thought of sharks and crocodiles, so one took an oar and another a paddle and every few seconds beat the water soundly. We all linked up with the cutter inside the sand-bar and managed to clamber aboard. We chugged up river for quite a time and it was a joy to experience the coolness of the tropical forest. Once or twice we passed a few natives, Papuans or New Guinean. I seem to remember the men wore their hair long and the women short. One of our chaps had brought a rifle with him but the only thing we had a pot at was a flying fox high above the trees. It was a big enough target but apparently he didn't hit it. I mentioned our fear of sharks and crocodiles: some of us recalled the unpleasant incident in Ceylon when we discovered that we were swimming in a lake occupied by crocodiles; half a dozen of them were lined up at the waters edge, like rowing boats, on a beach quite close to where we were. Sharks became a real fear at Manus. At first "hands

to bathe" meant almost half the ship's company went over-
board, until one evening the Petty Officers, the keen fish-
ermen, hauled up a shark. It was only a small one, of about
6 feet, but it was enough to put us off our daily swim. On
another occasion, in Sydney Harbour, the Petty Officers had
to arrange for the 4 ton crane to haul in-board a 490lb Ray
and I remember watching a large octopus suck its way from
port to starboard across the Quarter deck.

We eventually left Manus, sailed through the Bismarck
Sea, the Solomon Sea and the Coral Sea and a week later
arrived once again in Sydney for 3 months of Australian hos-
pitality and exciting experiences. Perhaps the most interesting was a week's stay on a sheep station in New South
Wales at a place called Molong, near to what might be called
the town of Orange. Mr McGill, our host, told us the station was somewhat rundown since his wife died; he thought
there were now only about 24,000 sheep. It was reckoned
that 4 sheep went to one acre of land. At that particular time
the land was in poor shape because there had been no rain
for some time and great cracks and crevices appeared all
over the place. My companion was Commander John Grace,
our gunnery officer and a relation of W G Grace. We were
supplied with a couple of horses and enjoyed a morning
ride around the station. Mr McGill had two other treasures
in addition to sheep; a very fine and up to date record play-
er and a wonderful collection of classical music records. He
explained that in the old days there was little else for one's
entertainment and as the nearest sheep station was probably some 20 miles away, parties were rare events. Nevertheless he had always made sure that his cellar was well
stocked. We both felt exceedingly jealous when he took us
down to the basement and let us in to have a look around.
We were a little dubious because the champagne we took
up stairs should obviously have been drunk some years
before, but the Napoleon brandy more than made up for
that. We wondered if he had any idea of what was in his cellar.

We were impressed by the sheep shearers, the speed and
the dexterity with which they carried out their job. I also
was impressed with the din made at night by the deep throat-
ed belches of the bull frogs.

It was during this stay in Sydney that I had my second frightening experience of the overwhelming power of the sea, when I thought my end had come. Yvonne, my Sydney girlfriend, had made up a picnic and went to the north shore, to Palm Beach. I wandered ahead and stood looking at the coral and the marine life in the pools. Quite suddenly with no warning at all a colossal wave crashed up over the rocks, knocked me down and as it receded dragged me nearer and nearer to the boiling cauldron of water many yards below. I knew if I was pulled into that I would not survive. I tried to grip the coral as I was pulled downwards and my arms and my legs and my back too were being torn pretty badly, but anything was better than being churned up in that seething mass of water below me. At length the receding water had drained off into the sea and I was able to scramble up off my back. The sea water made the bleeding look far worse than it was; my arms and legs were streaming and I walked into the sea thinking to wash it off, and then I thought of sharks and how they were supposed to be attracted by the smell, or taste, of blood and so I took to the dry sand. I expect the salt water was no bad thing for my cuts and scratches, some of which, especially on my arms, were quite deep and they were very sore indeed. I returned to the ship as quickly as I could and had them dressed in the sick bay. It was some weeks before they healed completely.

We used to enjoy visiting Taronga Park, the Zoo at Sydney and Luna Park, the fairground. An embarrassing experience occurred one evening when Yvonne and I were dining either at the Coq D'or or the Normandie Hotel in Sydney. We had finished the meal but before going on to a show we topped up with a liqueur. Mine was a Cherry Brandy which I promptly knocked over into my lap and all the wiping and rubbing with napkins couldn't remove the horrible stickiness which I had to live with through the show and the rest of the evening until I got back aboard. It was embarrassing in that one couldn't keep trying to ease one's trousers away from one's crutch!

On another evening I had gone ashore and was on my way into town when there was the most tremendous explosion. It seemed to come from the harbour and so I returned to Man-o-War steps to find that a war-head on a torpedo in one of our destroyers had fired taking some of the super structure with it and burning a rating very badly indeed. He had almost no skin left on him. I said a prayer with him because he was still just conscious and gave him God's blessing before he was taken to hospital. He died a few days later; thank goodness there was no other loss of life.

CHAPTER FOURTEEN

Japan

After three months of this pleasant stay in Sydney we sailed north, put in at Manus in the Admiralty Islands for a couple of nights and then off to Japan arriving in Yokohama harbour in time for Christmas 1945. We were impressed with the size of the harbour; it took about 20 minutes for the liberty boat to get in from the ship to the landing stage. The first Japanese I saw were the children who in their padded suits seemed to be as broad as they were tall. They ran up to us greeting us over and over again with the only English they appeared to know: "Allo, goobye". We found the adults very small compared with Europeans. The road from Yokohama to Tokyo, about 19 miles was a scene of terrible destruction. The Americans with their Flying Fortresses had left very little standing, apart from the most modern buildings which had been designed after the 1923 earthquake to stand up to future earthquakes, but much of the town had still been built of wood, paper and plaster. Shortly after arriving in Yokohama I took the opportunity of visiting Tokyo and was a bit put off by the behaviour of the American military police who followed our car the whole 19 miles to Tokyo. We were only too conscious of the limit – 20 miles per hour I think it was – and were determined not to be caught out, but inadvertently we may well have touched 21mph and in a flash the police car was in front of us waving us down and giving us a rollicking. When we got to Tokyo our first call was at the British Embassy to lodge a complaint at such treatment. We heard no more of it. On another occasion, coming back to Yokohama from Tokyo in a 15cwt truck in which there were 3 or 4 of us and some gear we had picked up, we had to stop at a crossroads. I was sitting uncomfortably at the rear of the truck holding on to the tail-board and side. I saw an American truck approaching and thought the driver was going a bit fast but concluded he would at any moment brake. He didn't and he hit us a terrifying blow, shooting us all on top of each other. Luckily we were not hurt, apart from some bruises. What remains clearly in my memory was my horror when I realised he wasn't going to stop. He could offer no explanation of his conduct.

Tokyo was a sorry sight in that winter of 1945-46. It seemed as if most of the 7 million inhabitants must have possessed bicycles and bivouacked in shacks made from beaten-out American petrol cans. It was a town of contrasts between old and new buildings and between modern western and traditional Japanese dress.

On the morning of Boxing Day I was invited by the Admiral to join a party on a picnic at a place some miles from Yokohama, Myanoshita, from which we had a breathtakingly beautiful view of Fujiyama. Everywhere was covered in snow. The Americans provided a powerful car that seated about six of us comfortably. It flew the British and American flags and had 5 stars up which meant that any Allied service man was pretty prompt in his salute. The Japanese weren't so aware of what all this razz-ma-tazz meant and on more than one occasion as we flashed through the villages, I thought we were about to mow down the crowds of Japanese because the American driver didn't slacken his pace for anything or anyone and his pace was considerable. We enjoyed an exceptionally good lunch and although we sat out in the open we didn't feel the cold. Close by, in the gardens of what must have been a 5-star hotel was a pond with the largest carp I have ever seen. They were of all colours and I can understand why they are so popular with the Japanese.

Another interesting trip was to the Kamakura Buddha 1291 AD, a huge bronze figure 41 feet high. I found he had a strange influence on me and I'm sure it wasn't only on me but on everyone who was prepared to stand and take in something of the peace and serenity of this figure. I understand he has been exercising this influence on people for the last 600 years.

A somewhat longer stay at Nikko was another never-to-be forgotten experience. It was some distance from Yokohama and the train journey was not too pleasant. About four of us squashed into cattle trucks with hundreds of

84

Japanese and found that once we were in, we stood with our arms to our sides unable to move. At each station we stopped at more and more people came aboard and we began to wonder what the limit was. However, towards the end of the journey I managed to get out and cadge a seat next to the driver of the train, an electric train, and it became an enjoyable journey from then on.

Nikko is fairly high up in the mountains and with the deep snow I found the air so freezingly cold that I had a job to breathe as I walked to the Hotel where we were to stay. The view early the next morning was a memorable one as the sun rose on the surrounding snow capped peaks as they appeared through the clouds, giving them a beautiful pinkish tint. Nikko is noted for its 31 or 32 Buddhist and Shinto Temples and shrines. The carvings on the fronts of the Temples, often animals and birds were all lacquered in reds and golds and blacks and they stood out so beautifully against the background of the deep white snow.

We were allowed into these shrines but had to remove our shoes first. I was just a little ashamed of the great holes fore and aft in my socks.

The first occasion we had trouble over the business of removing our shoes was when the Deep Sea Rover crew went to Atami for a short stay. About ten or a dozen, including the schoolie and myself thought we would get a taste of Japanese living by going to a Japanese style inn, rather than the western-American type of hotel. We had not more than set a foot inside the small reception area when there was the most appalling shouting and what seemed to us like screaming from the one or two girl receptionists. I was quite frightened and thought for the moment that we had come into the wrong entrance. They were pointing to our feet and then to the line of straw-like slippers. We at last realised we had to take off our shoes and put on the slippers. We were then allotted our room and asked if we would like a bath. We said "no thanks we had one quite recently". This wasn't accepted as sufficient reason for not bathing and we were taken along to the deep pool, steaming with water from the hot springs. We went back to our room and stripped off and after a good deal of hesitation and toe-dipping managed to get into the very hot bath. Usually when bathing the hesitation arises from the coldness of the water, this was a new experience for us all. Once in we quickly acquired the colour of boiled lobster and felt so utterly drained of energy that we were content to lie peacefully, like the three monkeys we had seen carved on one of the Temples at Nikko, seeing nothing, hearing nothing, saying nothing. I should think it was the nearest one would ever get to the Buddhist ideal of Nirvana. And then suddenly Paradise was lost by the entrance of two or three Japanese girls who slipped off their kimonos and stepped nude into the pool with ten nude men. Schoolie and I looked at each other as much as to say, "I think it's time we got out". We weren't going to be let off so easily; the girls got out and turned upside down some small wooden buckets and made us sit on them and then washed our backs for us. Apparently we should have had this treatment before we entered the pool. It was all good clean fun.

Supper time was fun too. We felt we should adopt the orthodox position and so knelt back on our heels at the low tables about 8" above ground level. All went well for a while but it wasn't long before one of the party felt an irresistible urge to change his position to avoid the cramp he knew was upon him. This desire for change was infectious and it wasn't long before each of us was sitting, kneeling or standing in the position he found suited best his ability to manage his food.

The Rover crew contained the inevitable cockney wit or two and the episode of the bathing followed by the supper party had prepared us for the most hilarious event of the day: the preparation for the night. The Japanese girl appeared not to understand when we asked where our bedrooms were. We were shown a pile of huge mattresses and we gathered these had to be laid on the floor of our room. We asked where the sheets and blankets were and was each given a huge padded dressing gown about 3 feet longer than the wearer, somewhat like a modern duvet. We stripped off our clothes and wrapped these gowns around us. The problem now was how to lie down on one's mattress: it was impossible to walk without tripping up, which we did again and again, but we experimented and found the only thing to do was to position oneself at the foot of the mattress and to fall as gently as possible on to one's back and hope it was vaguely the right place. Actually with the soaking in the hot-spring water and the incessant laughter at supper and at bedtime we all slept exceedingly well.

I suppose the most vivid memory of the time we spent in Japan was our visit, first to Hiroshima and then to Nagasaki. I found it difficult to believe that the utter devastation of such a vast area that was Hiroshima, was caused by one small bomb. There were a number of streams or canals, criss-crossing the town and some had chains running alongside them and I remember tracing on the tarmac of the road what one might refer to as the reflection of the posts and the chains where the heat and intense light of the bomb had silhouetted them. There was also the outline of a man with a horse and cart and a dog. It was an uncanny picture. I managed to get a Jesuit priest to come aboard to give a first-hand account of the atom bomb which wiped out Hiroshima and many thousands of its inhabitants and left many more thousands burned and charred and doomed for life.

Nagasaki contained the great industrial complex of Mitsubishi. The steel girders that were left standing were all curved like hawthorn trees exposed to the prevailing wind on the top of the hill. In another part of the town hundreds of large trees lay in neat rows just as if lumberjacks had felled them and laid them in parallel lines. The thing which impressed me most was the little pile of china, most of it broken into small pieces which was obviously the contents of the china cupboard in each of the houses. A pile was to be seen every so many feet apart down the entire length of a street. The only glass to be found was that which had melted on to bits of china or which looked like a flat pancake of wax. I found bits of newspaper sandwiched between pieces of china, or between china and melted glass. Where the factories had been there was a good deal of iron and steel turnings all fused into lumps. In one corner of Nagasaki there was a small hill which had protected a few houses and shops from the impact of the bomb which had destroyed the town from the sea straight up the valley. It was from a shop there that I bought a number of Japanese prints, most of them about 100 years old.

Our visit to Hiroshima took us through the Inland Sea;

two memories of that stand out. First the most beautiful *The ruins of Hiroshima* scenery and then of the many scuttled Japanese battleships at Kure which reminded one of the bottoms of the German battleships at Scapa Flow. We put in at Kagoshima, a naval base at the southern end of Kyushu. We were lying under the shadow of a volcano Sakura Shimo 3661ft which every 11 minutes made a rather frightening rumbling noise but after a while we got used to it and carried on regardless especially as we were assured by the Japanese that there was nothing to it. It was there that the RC Padre and I went ashore one Saturday afternoon to visit the Naval barracks. He seemed to have some influential friend there and we were invited to choose ourselves a Japanese sword each. Room after room was stacked from floor to ceiling with swords, all surrendered by Japanese naval officers. Some were quite modern, all gilt and glitter, others were shabby but genuine 200-300 years old Samurai swords. The sword-smith selected one for me and told me he could tell it was about 250 years old because of the silver band round the top of the blade. We both felt a certain sense of guilt because we knew that the acquiring of Japanese officers' swords by the RN was forbidden. But it gave us a nice sense of one-upman-

88

Nagasaki: The town lay in a valley, with hills on either side,- this probably increased the effect of the atom bomb

ship and after all it was so easy. The difficulty was how to get them back aboard. We came to the conclusion that the best hiding place was down the leg of our trousers. This meant we both limped slightly, but nothing to worry about until we had to step down from the jetty into the liberty boat. We managed. Then came the real test getting aboard our ship, climbing up the long sloping gangway of many steps. The foot work wasn't too difficult because we had one good leg; the other one at times could be awkward and it meant that both Padres came aboard limping and clutching their stomachs; there was no other way to stop the swords slipping down. It wasn't until after church the next morning when we were just about to sail away from Kagoshima that we took our prizes down to the Wardroom. We were not popular, but were the centre of envy. Many years later I sold my acquisition for £190.

CHAPTER FIFTEEN

Homeward Bound

With the approach of demobilization of many ratings in the Pacific Fleet I found when visiting the mess decks of the Destroyers that men were a bit lost as to what to do with the Yen they still had, especially if they knew they weren't likely to get ashore again before setting off for home. I told them that I wanted to buy some pearls for a wedding present for my wife-to-be but that I had no hope of finding the thousands of yen required. They were only too pleased to find a worthy cause and it wasn't long before I was able to go to the Captain of our ship and ask him that the next time he visited the Ginza, the Harrods of Tokyo – to buy me a string of pearls. The pearls apparently were obtainable on a floor restricted to high ranking officers only. Should anyone think the Padre acted at all shamefully in accepting Yen from the mess decks perhaps I should explain that many men were rolling in Yen. They used to use their ration of ticklers, cigarette tobacco, to roll a few hundred cigarettes and then pack them neatly in soap or toothpaste cartons or any small boxes or containers, seal them with sticky paper, take them ashore and flog them at a colossal profit. I had no compunction about accepting a bit of the rake-off. I forget now the cost of that pearl necklace, but it was many thousands of yen.

One of my regular jobs, with other officers, was the censoring of letters. It was a bit of a burden at times when there was a deadline for the collection of mail before the ship sailed but it was for me a joy to find that for every broken marriage there must have been hundreds that were holding fast. It was the regular visiting of the mess decks that now and again brought to light problems that would not otherwise have been shared with the Chaplain, especially in the destroyers that were in company in harbour. Not all destroyer flotillas had their own Padre and when these were tied up alongside in harbour for maintenance or repairs I tried to spend as much time as possible with them and to invite some of their officers aboard for a drink or for dinner. I remember one evening in Trincomalee having a gin with the 1st Lieutenant of HMS *Whelp*, Prince Philip. I asked him if he was getting any leave and he said he was spending a week with his uncle. "Oh", I said, "you have an uncle out here?" "Yes, Lord Louis". I felt a bit stupid.

The Chaplain wasn't officially appointed as Welfare Officer but that was reckoned as one of the hats he wore and this covered Entertainment. A lot depended on whether the ship's company were keen on getting up concerts. We were fortunate in this respect especially as we carried a large number of officers, some of whom brought ideas from shows they had taken part in in former ships and some who were most efficient producers of first class concerts. We managed to put on some really good programmes.

At one ship's concert, a revue entitled, 'Pacifically Yours', I took part in an act which I enjoyed immensely: it was an elaboration of something I had put on at Theological College, but liberalized somewhat: "In a Persian Market". It gave lots of scope for jugglers, snake charmers, dancing girls and all sorts of characters. Two other officers, John Grace, George Millburn, as well as I had quite presentable beards, which then were by no means as fashionable as they are today. According to the programme they were supplied by Grace Wallisburn. With coatings of cocoa, turbans and very economic loin cloths we sat crossed legged in a row at the front of the stage, facing the front row of the audience, the Admiral and the top brass. We were described in the programme as beggars and between our attempts to hum the musical score of 'In a Persian Market', we were chewing beetle nut and every so often felt the urge to imitate the natives in the easy way they half-spat, or rather squirted, the beetle juice quite some distance. The officers in the front row did not appreciate this act half as much as the members of the lower deck. The Press Reviews, printed on the backs of the programmes, contained: 'I have never seen anything like it' – Mail; 'I enjoyed the interval' – Telegraph.

At last a berth was found for me to begin my homeward trip. It was in HMS *Apollo*, a mine layer. We put into Hong

Kong and I spent an evening ashore in the Peninsula Hotel at Kowloon where for dinner I sat at a table with a Colonel Pittendright, Superintendent of Hong Kong Water Police. He shared with me what he said was a bottle of sherry. I've never drunk methylated spirits or neat vinegar before, but I reckon this could have been a blend of the two. The evening went well until some hours later I was standing on the jetty waiting for a boat to take me back to the ship which was standing some way off. The conviction became strong that I was shortly to be ill. I managed to get aboard and to find the heads just in time. The next day I transferred to another mine layer, HMS *Ariadne*. My wife-to-be had laid down a condition: she would marry me provided I got shot of my beard. So the first morning in HMS *Ariadne* with great regret I shaved it off. I was somewhat surprised when later in the morning the 1st Lieutenant told me the Captain wanted to see me. I duly reported to him and he tore me off a strip for not requesting permission to shave off. I was taken aback and said that as I'd never requested permission to

On the way home, HMS Ariadne.

grow a set, I felt there was no need to request permission to shave off.

The leisurely trip home at 15 knots from Singapore with calls at Aden, Malta and Gibraltar was a grand finale to my short Naval career. We all enjoyed ourselves immensely with constant swimming in the canvas pool rigged on the quarter deck and with bridge and poker – dice in the Ward Room and cribbage on the mess decks. I must have spent many hours playing cribbage, not only in my own ship but in the destroyers for whom we were responsible. I found it a natural way in to a relationship with men who wouldn't normally have had much to do with, or to say to a Parson. The only time we played bridge with any regularity was when it was too hot to think of getting any sleep before the early hours, when we were at Manus in the Admiralty Islands, or the Marshall Islands or in the Philippines. The school usually consisted of the Admiral, the Paymaster Captain, the PMO and myself. The extraordinary thing is that since the day I arrived at Plymouth, St George's Day 1946, I haven't played a single game of bridge. I think the reasoning was that if it were known in a parish that the Rector played bridge he might often be called to make up a four and would certainly feel a sense of guilt if, having accepted one invitation, he declined another. Added to which it can be too time consuming when one is a busy man.

One morning on the way between Ceylon and Aden I was awakened by a rating thrusting a signal pad in front of me. The signal read "Proceed all speed Abadan". I hadn't a clue where Abadan was; my only thought was: does this mean we shan't get home after all? I immediately proceeded with all speed to the Wardroom and found all the officers had done the same. All were asking "where is Abadan?" Someone mentioned the Persian Gulf and then most of us remembered that there had been a spot of trouble there about oil. Morale was very low indeed that morning. Most of us had been overseas for a year or two and joy at the thought of getting home within the next few weeks suddenly went out of the port hole and in its place came anger, hatred and malice against all who conducted the affairs of the Royal Navy. I don't know what it was that suddenly switched our attention from maps and charts of the Arabian Sea, the Gulf of Oman and the Persian Gulf to Pilot. I suppose it was only to be expected that he should know where Abadan was and how long it would take us to reach there but he had been somewhat subdued when everyone else was letting off a good deal of steam. Quite out of the blue someone said "What's the date?" It was April 1st. Pilot of course was the perpetrator. He was lucky to get away with his life. His wine bill took a considerable battering but we all agreed after an hour or two of near despair that it wasn't a bad joke after all.

At Aden we had a run ashore and braved the appalling stink of Old Aden to visit the Queen of Sheba's water tanks. I bought a couple of Persian rugs which are still doing good service. I was impressed by the man who sold them to me: I hadn't with me anything like the cash required but when I asked if he would take a cheque he at once said: "Of course Sir, you are a Naval Officer". A similar attitude had been taken by the man in Colombo who sold me a sapphire ring. Unfortunately the English customs were not so accommodating when we disembarked at Plymouth on St George's Day: What with Japanese pearls and prints and lacquer ware, Persian rugs and the ring from Ceylon and sundry bottles from Soccone and Speed and many other bits and pieces.

It was Holy Week when we put into Malta and the season of religious processions. I was asked to be in charge of a lad who was returning from holidays to Gresham's School in Norfolk and to see him as far as London. He had been great fun and the ship's company enjoyed having him aboard. I retain one or two vivid memories of him: Sunday evenings after dinner the wardroom always had a film and most officers enjoyed a cigar. On this particular Sunday the lad had dined with us and came to the film with a cigar going on each side of him. It was also a bit of a choppy side. After some time and after one or two audible sighs he whispered to me "Padre I think I might be sick". We picked our way out and up on to the deck where the fresh air helped a bit and we found our way to the writer's small office where his camp bed was. He got into his pyjamas and knelt down to say his prayers but a lurch of the ship put him off balance. I told him that I thought the Good Lord would understand if he called prayers off for that night.

94

We at length arrived at Plymouth on St George's Day 1946, a little fed up that we had to walk across another ship, I think it was HMS *Gambia*, to get ashore but there was a mass of shipping there. Most of us spent the night in Plymouth before setting off the next morning for London. I felt a little sad to say farewell to HMS *Ariadne*, and to the Navy in general.

As we boarded the train at North End the lad joined my fiancee and me, very concerned about a huge bunch of bananas he was taking back to school with him. Before the train actually started he got out and ran along to the guard's van to make sure the bananas were aboard. I can't remember how many times the train stopped, no more than once or twice but the same routine was adopted at each stop. He had to be sure the bunch of bananas was still with him.

I'm only too conscious that most of these recollections bear little relation to the work of a Naval Chaplain. They might well be descriptions of a lengthy cruise and of the places visited and of the experiences one was privileged to enjoy. In case any reader should get the impression that it was all one long holiday and all fun and games perhaps I should go into a little more detail of the Chaplain's activities on board.

I have already mentioned that in HMS *Tyne* we began each day with a service of Holy Communion and I was able to keep a roster of servers going so that there were always a few of us present. I'm glad to say the Roman Catholics, with Monsignor Elwes, were happy to use the chapel for mass on Sundays and week days. There were classes of preparation for Confirmation, sometimes just a single candidate, sometimes a group of 4 or 5 men. A good deal depended on where and when we could lay hands on a Bishop. It was all right at Scapa where the Bishop of Argyll and The Isles was available. When we were in the Philippines I heard that a Bishop from the Solomon Islands was around. I managed to trace him only to find he was not an Anglican but an American Methodist Bishop which I didn't know existed.

One of the two duties laid on a Chaplain in KR & AI (Kings Regulations and Admiralty Instructions) was a visit to the Sick Bay each day. It wasn't often that men were seriously ill; they were often bored with lying in their cots and so a visit and a chat was appreciated. The other duty was to visit the occupants of the cells. When we were at sea there weren't so many as when we were in harbour. I think the Padre's visit was appreciated because life was not much fun cooped up in a minute cell with a Bible only for reading material, and that of the old-fashioned small type which I always felt was enough to stop anyone attempting to read it. Then of course there was Oakum picking; a more useless activity one could scarcely imagine. It may have been all right for the first hour or two but after the first day or two when one's finger tips began to get sore it became what it was supposed to be – a punishment. I was able to take a book in now and again if a man was willing to read a bit of religion. Sometimes one was asked to write to a wife in order to sort out a relationship that was apparently getting out of hand and this applied to other members of the ship's company and not only to those in cells. I found that it wasn't always the sailor husband who was to blame for an upset marriage, the sailor's wife could be the cause of a lot of misery to a man on the other side of the world.

After five years as a Naval Chaplain I came to the conclusion that it is not so much what a Chaplain does or does not do, as what he is. Years before I had ever thought of being ordained let alone becoming a Service Chaplain, I was impressed by the way a cousin of mine who had served in the Sappers in the 1914-18 War spoke so glowingly of the Chaplain of his Unit. Later I came across a number of service men who had nothing but good to say of their Padres. This struck me as being somewhat different from the general attitude of people towards their parish priests. I don't think Chaplains are particularly good or holy men; they are like most parish priests, men who try to love and serve God and who try to love and serve their fellow men. But it is because they live so close to their fellow men, especially those who serve in the parochial confines of a ship, that they are seen and known to be perfectly normal human beings and the men who serve with them are so impressed, relieved perhaps, that the parson is human and not sanctimonious, as for some reason they've imagined most clerics to be, that their response is to accept him and to give him more respect than they would to the vicar of a parish.

Of course many members of a ship's company don't get further than that, some don't even get that far and don't give the Padre a thought but generally speaking the Chaplain is accepted for what he is and is known to be.

CHAPTER SIXTEEN

From Naval Padre to College Chaplain

Having exchanged hundreds of air mail letters and having bought a sapphire engagement ring in Colombo, I eventually proposed marriage and was accepted by air mail so that after my arrival back in the United Kingdom we lost as little time as possible. We were married on my fiancee's birthday, 4th May, at the village of Hilperton on the outskirts of Trowbridge by Padre John Armstrong with whom I had served in the Royal Marines and who later became Chaplain of the Fleet. There were a few Royal Marine Commandos there including my best man and a large enough Naval contingent to form a Guard of Honour but I must confess I got a bit rattled with them all when eventually I tried to drive away in the two-seater bull-nosed Morris with all the paraphernalia they had attached: kettle, saucepan, tin cans, etc. For some weeks afterwards confetti and paper rose petals would float up from the depths of the car when the hood was lowered.

We stayed the first night of our honeymoon at Salisbury because I was to see the Bishop on the Monday morning about a possible parish. I was surprised when he came up with four or five possibles and the one we decided to go to look at was Allington St Swithun at Bridport. The Bishop had only that morning received the resignation of the incumbent and the latter was shaken to the core on the morning of his day off to receive a visit from a couple sent by the Bishop to look at the parish. We fell for it, sent an acceptance to the Bishop, and got on with our honeymoon in Devonshire. It wasn't until September that we eventually moved in so slowly do the wheels turn. Meanwhile I did a locum at West Moors for a few weeks, helped at the parish where I had been curate, played a good deal of tennis and generally enjoyed life back in England. We thoroughly enjoyed our time at Allington in Bridport; it was a grand parish but we spent only two years there.

While I was somewhere in the Pacific I had received a suggestion that I apply for the chaplaincy of my College at Durham University. As it was for a single man to live in, and I knew I was to be married on my return to England I didn't even acknowledge the letter. In the summer of 1947 we went to Durham for June Week and the June Ball and a number of people wondered why I had not applied for the post in 1946. Actually the man who had been appointed decided after his two years probationary period that he did not wish to stay on. This gave me a second chance but I was undecided: we were happy where we were but a college chaplaincy and Durham itself were tremendous attractions; on the other hand, we were living in a lovely rectory with a large garden and, believe it or not, with a part-time gardener who would not take more than a shilling an hour. Our rooms in Durham would be in a building about 300 years old and not very convenient or manageable. In addition, I would have to do a certain amount of coaching in Latin and Greek and I felt that I had forgotten what little I had ever known. However, after consulting one or two friends I applied, was short-listed, and appointed. I then had to inform the Bishop. He was furious with me for not consulting him first and tore me off such a strip that I went home and was physically ill for a couple of days. I had never been reprimanded so heartily in my life before. I had worked on the assumption that, had I consulted him, he would most probably have put pressure on me to remain where I was and, had I made the move in spite of his advice, I should have been in trouble anyway so I felt it best to get the job and then inform the Bishop. I thought, at the time, that I had ruined my chances of ever getting back into Salisbury Diocese again – but Bishops change.

We took up residence in Durham in September, 1948. Most of the undergraduates were ex-Service types and it was a joy to be with them. After a year or so we received our first schoolboy and it wasn't long before all new intakes were straight from school.

My chaplaincy duties were by no means confined to chapel services, although with two College chapels to serve

99

– one in University College in Durham Castle and one in Hatfield College, I had to get some clerical help which wasn't difficult. The retired Vice-Master of Hatfield, Dr Pace, was only too willing and happy to be of assistance, as was the tutor in Science, Dr Gregory, and other members of staff.

I tried to keep a rule of being in chapel at 7.15 each morning for my own prayers and then at 8am on two mornings a week a service of Holy Communion in one or other of the chapels and then we would say morning prayer at 8.30 each day so that people could get to lectures at 9am.

On Fridays we would say the Litany. Dr Pace became increasingly deaf over the years and one Friday morning his deafness produced a certain amount of mirth. Those who know about such things will appreciate that to say Morning Prayer, plus the Litany, would take all of half an hour or so. To shorten things I used to omit the Creed and all that followed in Morning Prayer and go straight into the Litany with a brief warning to that effect. On one particular Friday morning it was obvious that Dr Pace wasn't hearing too well or hadn't properly adjusted his hearing aid because when I gave the usual warning, "We shall now say the Litany", Dr Pace, in his deep lugubrious voice, came out with, "Christ have mercy upon us". After forty years, rather naughtily, I still find that incident funny.

Another amusing incident occurred one evening in chapel. The Old Testament lesson was the story of Samson and Delilah and we had just heard how Delilah had bound Samson with seven new ropes and then had told him that the Philistines were upon him: 'And he brake them off his arms like a thread'. At this moment, with perfect timing, a starling up in the eves of the chapel roof let out a piercing whistle expressing either amazement, incredulity or envy, and producing laughter in the congregation.

Michael Ramsay, before he went to Cambridge as Regius Professor of Theology, was one of the Canon professors at Durham. When he was appointed Bishop of Durham he lived for some weeks in Durham Castle while Auckland Castle was being renovated. I was glad of his help in chapel but he was a bit forgetful and one evening I was just about to begin evensong in the Castle Chapel when there was a noisy entry, and I looked up to see Michael Ramsay standing there looking a bit lost. I still feel conscience-stricken when I remember whispering to him from my stall, "You're in the other place." He humbly shut the chapel door and began his five-minute walk to Hatfield College Chapel.

Each college had its organ scholar and with a flourishing music school at the University to draw on, the standard of singing at the Christmas Carol Services and at the concerts of madrigals was high. One of the pleasantest memories of chapel events was of the fortnightly Eucharists on Sunday mornings, followed by breakfast in my rooms, a tremendous squash but a source of a real sense of fellowship. In the vacations I enjoyed taking Sunday services in the mining villages of County Durham. I spent many afternoons coaching on the river and quite early in my chaplaincy found a really first-class crew which proved unbeatable and I had the pleasure of taking them to row against Edinburgh University and so to repeat the experience I had enjoyed some dozen years before.

After nine years I found I was becoming critical of some of the young gentlemen and felt it was probably time I moved back to parish life. I hadn't a clue what I wanted to do or where I wanted to go, and then one day out of the blue came a letter from a church warden in a village suggesting I come to look at the parish of four small hamlets, deep in the heart of Dorset.

CHAPTER SEVENTEEN

Deep in the Heart of Dorset

In the Easter vacation we often used to spend some time with my wife's sister in Wiltshire and, as we were not far from Dorset, I went to have a look at the four little villages. Unfortunately one of our two young daughters had measles so my wife did not accompany me. Had she done so I doubt if we should have made the move. The total population of the four was under 300; the rectory stood in about 2 acres of land; there were 31 apple trees in the orchard; the large lawn consisted of grass about three feet high and the double-laurel walks and the many beech and privet hedges were at least twice as high as they should have been. There had been no incumbent for the past twelve months. The house was far better than the accommodation we had occupied for the past nine years in Durham but it was cut off from the village, but with only a field in between, it stood next to a pub.

I was torn and found it most difficult to make a decision. Some members of the Senior Common Room thought I must be mad to consider taking such a small rural job and I almost agreed and yet there was a challenge in it. If I should turn it down because I felt it was beneath me, so to speak, and because I felt I should take on a larger populous town parish somewhere, then I should be refusing to accept the challenge.

After a good deal of heart searching I accepted and we moved back to Dorset and to Salisbury Diocese. The Bishop, who nine years before had taken such a dim view of my movements, had died and the Right Reverend William Anderson welcomed me; he, too, had served as a Naval Chaplain.

Our first job was to try to get the wilderness of the garden into some sort of shape. It was great fun and we were fortunate to be able to offer some of the Durham undergraduates free holidays in exchange for a bit of hard labour.

*The Church at Winter-
bourne Zelstone*

Ever since a child I've enjoyed bonfires but those we now had were out of this world. We went mechanized and bought a large motor mower, a rotary rough cutter, and a rotovator.

The busiest time was apple-picking. We had quite a bit of stabling and a loft where we could store the better Coxes and Bramleys. We had one very large Bramley apple tree which I used to climb with a bucket with a hook on its handle to hang it on a branch. It was lifting full buckets off branches which gave me two of the most excruciatingly painful tennis elbows: I couldn't lift the receiver from the telephone or even pass the mustard at table. Finally, the doctor gave me injections of cortisone between the bones in the elbows which I think was the most painful experience of my life.

I suppose one of the most useful acts of my time in these

hamlets was the founding of a village social club. In one of the villages there was a church school whose numbers had dropped to such an extent that it was to be closed. There was no pub in this village. Most of the men were forestry or agricultural workers and when a chap was thirsty he had to walk or get on his bike and make his way to the nearest pub a few miles away. I began making enquiries about the ecclesiastical and legal possibilities of converting the church school into a village club and getting a licence for the sale of liquor. It took some time but eventually the village had its family club and a few years ago my wife and I were invited to its 25th anniversary party.

After four years it was suggested I might consider moving into the neighbouring parish of Wareham. Although I had enjoyed my rural experience I felt that I was spending a little too much time gardening and gathering fruit and vegetables and that perhaps I ought to be stretched a little more and indeed was for the next eighteen years.

Wareham: The Big Job

I felt very privileged to be appointed as Rector of Wareham; it was a fairly important parish, a Dorset county market town, emerging from its quiet seclusion of the past. Ecclesiastically, it had taken under its wing various outlying districts which had formerly enjoyed parochial status. In a sense it was one of the earliest attempts at a team ministry. The rector had two assistant curates to help him look after the town of Wareham with two churches: Lady St Mary, and St Martin's, and to the south of the town St Nicholas at Arne, some three or four miles away, and the church at Creech. In addition there was an old folks' home which had a service each Sunday afternoon and Holy Communion monthly, and some ancient almshouses where prayers were said each Friday morning. Then there were three or four schools of which the rector was chairman of the managers of three and where he attempted to teach in two. To the north of the town was the separate district of Sandford served by the senior curate; it had originated as a row of cottages built to house the folk who worked in Sandford Pottery. It had its own church primary school but no church and so the school hall was used on Sundays for this purpose.

In the 1960s the intervening land was developed and new estates grew up almost overnight, bringing the population of the parish near to ten thousand. It was a busy and an exacting parish and on more than one occasion during my eighteen years as Rector, when I was short of staff, the pressure became a bit much. One of my first jobs was to build a parish hall: the rectory was used for every meeting. The parochial church council which usually numbered about 25 and met each month would have to walk over the gravel of the drive into the hall and the sitting room and if it had been raining the 25 pairs of boots and shoes produced a good deal of mud. The Mothers Union, the Young Wives

Sarah, John, Ruth and Jane at Wareham in 1962

Group, and various committees all met in the sitting room and I think our two young daughters were put off rectory life by frequently being told to be quiet in their bedrooms because this or that meeting was taking place downstairs. They eventually went away to boarding school but the need for a parish hall remained. A stewardship campaign was organised by the firm of Planned Giving and although the main event, the parish supper, took place at the height of the 1962 freeze-up, about 400 parishioners managed to get to the gymnasium at Bovington Camp and the income of the parish was raised from £5,000 per annum to £15,000.

Land adjoining the parish church had been given for a

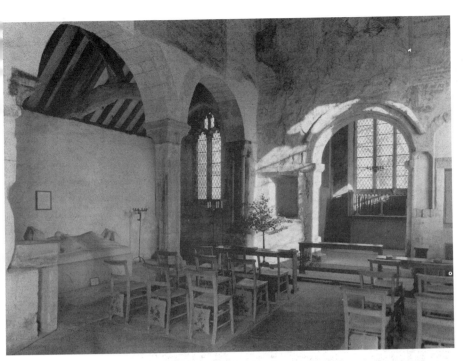

St Martin's Wareham, on the left of the picture is the effigy of T.E. Lawrence.

hall in 1932 and an architect had drawn up plans and quotations had been received for just over £2,000 to provide a hall and a caretaker's flat but, because the site was on a slight slope, one end being about five feet higher than the opposite end, it was reckoned that this made it impossible to build on the site and so no hall was produced. Actually, in 1962 a bulldozer came in one afternoon and in two days the site was levelled and a hall was built by the end of the year.

I noticed a great change taking place in the 1960s. When I went to Wareham in 1961 congregations were good. Mothering Sunday was especially well-attended by families coming in on coaches from all the outlying districts. Confirmations numbered between 50 and 60. On Ash Wednesday the parish church was crammed full with all the schools attending. I can't remember now which year the Forsyte Saga appeared on television on Sunday evenings but this was certainly when the Sunday evening congregations dropped and never recovered. I, unfortunately, fell between the devil and the deep blue sea when I took the view that if you can't beat them you join them and put evensong on at 5.30pm instead of 6.30pm thinking it would enable people to worship and to watch but I was accused by some of pandering to these modern tastes. I think I probably underestimated the sanctity of the Sunday tea. As the number of young confirmation candidates dropped, older candidates increased and over the years unlike so many of the younger ones, these communicants, with few exceptions, remained faithful.

There was a good deal of contact with the Junior Leaders' Regiment at Bovington. They were given the Freedom of the Borough of Wareham and each year they paraded and marched through the town to the parish church of Lady St Mary. I was happy to discover on moving to Wareham that the Commanding Officer, Royal Marines, Poole, lived in a house in my parish and over the years was very fortunate to be invited, both at his home and at their Mess in Poole, to meet officers with whom I had served during the war. I was also invited to stay the weekend and to preach at the Headquarters of 41 Royal Marine Commando at Bickleigh in Devonshire. It was a great joy in 1968 to take my wife and daughters to Bickleigh on Salerno Day, the 25th anniversary of our landing at Salerno.

Journey's End

Towards the end of the 1970s I began to feel that it was time I gave way to a younger man and in the summer of 1979 we retired to a bungalow in Blandford. I found it a tremendous wrench to leave Wareham after eighteen very happy years. I soon found that retirement is almost an impossibility for an Anglican priest and most Sundays I visited some parish or other where help was needed. In 1986 we moved to Wimborne Minster where a few years before I had served part-time for three months when their rector had retired, and for some years now I have been helping on a regular basis of two Sundays a month at Horton, near Wimborne.

On 19th May, 1990, I had completed fifty years as a priest in the Church of England. I hadn't thought in terms of making anything of it but some folk felt otherwise and, as a consequence, at a Eucharist in Witchampton Church, where I sometimes helped the Archdeacon of Dorset, there were about 120 fellow pilgrims from all the parishes and walks of life in which I had served. I was to have the chance of a chat at lunch afterwards with some of my fellow curates and with so many friends one hadn't seen for years and I was glad my wife had overruled my stubbornness and laid on such a wonderful anniversary celebration.

The words of the motto of University College, Durham, from Psalm 115, kept going through my mind, "Non nobis, Domine, non nobis" – "not unto us, O Lord, not unto us" – but the Psalm continues "but unto Thy Name give the praise for Thy loving mercy and for Thy truth's sake" and I would add, "for this wonderful life and my earthly pilgrimage and ministry, full of all sorts of experiences, of all sorts of people, in all sorts of circumstances."

CHAPTER NINETEEN

Footnote

After retirement John and Ruth lived for seven years in a bungalow in Blandford before moving to a listed cottage in Wimborne where John was able to enjoy peace and contentment. Ruth created a beautiful, colourful garden which gave them both infinite pleasure. After a short illness John died on 13th December, 1992.

R.F.